Christa Watson

HOW DO I *Quilt* IT?

LEARN MODERN MACHINE QUILTING

Using Walking-Foot & Free-Motion Techniques

stash BOOKS®

an imprint of C&T Publishing

Text and artwork copyright © 2022 by Christa Watson

Artwork copyright © 2022 by C&T Publishing, Inc.

PUBLISHER: Amy Barrett-Daffin

CREATIVE DIRECTOR: Gailen Runge

ACQUISITIONS EDITOR: Roxane Cerda

MANAGING EDITOR: Liz Aneloski

EDITOR: Beth Baumgartel

TECHNICAL EDITOR: Del Walker

COVER/BOOK DESIGNER: April Mostek

PRODUCTION COORDINATOR: Zinnia Heinzmann

ILLUSTRATOR: Aliza Shalit

SUBJECTS PHOTOGRAPHY by Lauren Herberg of C&T Publishing, Inc., unless otherwise noted

PHOTOGRAPHY ASSISTANT: Gabriel Martinez

COVER AND INSTRUCTIONAL PHOTOGRAPHY by Susanne Shultis, unless otherwise noted

Published by Stash Books, an imprint of C&T Publishing, Inc., P.O. Box 1456, Lafayette, CA 94549

Library of Congress Cataloging-in-Publication Data

Names: Watson, Christa, author.
Title: How do I quilt it? : learn modern machine quilting using walking-foot and free-motion techniques / Christa Watson.
Description: Lafayette, CA : Stash Books, [2022] | Summary: "Readers will learn how to create a quilting plan and learn quilting techniques. Includes various quilting designs and 3 quilt projects to practice skills"-- Provided by publisher.
Identifiers: LCCN 2022004686 | ISBN 9781644030806 (trade paperback) | ISBN 9781644030813 (ebook)
Subjects: LCSH: Machine quilting. | Machine quilting--Technique. | Machine quilting--Patterns.
Classification: LCC TT835 .W375926 2022 | DDC 746.46/041--dc23/eng/20220207
LC record available at https://lccn.loc.gov/2022004686

Printed in the USA

10 9 8 7 6 5 4 3 2 1

DEDICATION

To my family—thank you for putting up with me during the writing of this book. You've all been my biggest supporters and cheerleaders, especially during crazy times.

ACKNOWLEDGMENTS

Thanks to Hobbs Bonded Fibers for providing all of the batting, to Aurifil for providing the thread, and to Benartex for providing all of the quilt fabric to make the projects in this book. All quilts were designed by Christa using Electric Quilt software. They were pieced and quilted by the author on a BERNINA 770QE. Thanks to Arrow Cabinets for collaborating to produce the Christa Sewing Cabinet, available wherever fine sewing furniture is sold. Thanks to Susanne Shultis Photography for all the pictures taken in studio.

Contents

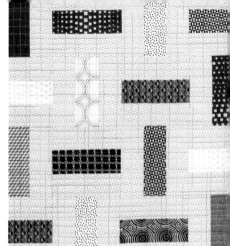

Embracing Imperfection

I like to call myself a perfectly imperfect quilter. That's because I'm a *recovering* perfectionist. Back in the mid-90s when I began quilting, I wanted to make the best quilts I could, but I stressed too much about perfection. I saw beautiful quilt show-quality quilts in magazines and would get frustrated thinking I could never make them. After all, I had only been quilting for a short time back then, and these amazing, nationally award-winning quilters had been quilting for their entire lives. How could I compare?

A few years later, as a mom with young children, I still loved my amazing quilting hobby, but I was short on time. I continued to admire the knock-your-socks-off "Best of Show" type quilts, but I didn't have the 400 (thousand) hours it would take to make one. So, I did the next best thing—I began to design and make quick, easy quilts that I DID have time for: those quilts with interesting geometric shapes made from simple pieced blocks. I could show off some really fun fabrics in my quilts AND mask my imperfections with dense, textural quilting.

Because I didn't know any other options existed, I machine quilted all of my own quilts on a regular home sewing machine, figuring the only way I knew I'd get better was by making more quilts! Along the way, I developed a few tricks to help hide my mistakes without being too obvious. And you know what? As I gained confidence in my skills, I decided to enter a few of those imperfect quilts into shows. I even picked up a ribbon or two along the way.

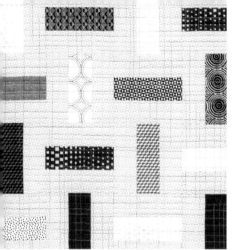

I've also had the honor of judging a few quilt shows and have witnessed near-perfection up close and personal. But when given a choice, I tend to gravitate to those quirky quilts where you can definitely see the hand of the maker, over computerized perfection, any day!

As I began teaching my "perfectly imperfect" methods over the years, more and more students embraced my techniques. During class they all breathed a big sigh of relief once they realized they could make stunning quilts that didn't have to be perfect to be functional and beautiful.

This philosophy aligns well with the modern quilting movement, in which I've fallen head over heels for in the last few years. The day I ditched my intricately carved machine quilting stencils and embraced a more organic, irregular stitching style, was a happy day indeed!

As you read the pages of this book and try out some of the projects and techniques, I hope you'll let go of perfection and enjoy the process. I give you permission to try new things, to make mistakes, to learn something you haven't done before, and most of all to *have fun* doing it!

— Christa

Photo by C&T Publishing, Inc.

GETTING *Started*

To answer the often-asked query, "How do I quilt this?" we need to explore the following two questions in more detail: (1) How do I physically quilt my quilt? and (2) What designs should I choose? The scope of this book is from a domestic (sit-down) machine quilting perspective, but many of the ideas and techniques can be adapted to longarm quilting as well.

My simple answer to both questions is to choose fun and forgiving walking-foot designs; carefree, yet interesting free-motion quilting; or to feature both techniques in the same quilt! The options may depend on how much time you have, your current skill level, as well as the intended recipient. But the great news about learning the techniques presented in this book is that you'll get faster, better, and more comfortable with the process with each quilt you make.

In the pages that follow, I demonstrate how to prepare your quilt for stress-free stitching, determine the best quilting path around the quilt, and divide and conquer the tasks in the most efficient way possible. I'll also show how to make a quilting plan that will help you decide whether you want to quilt a quick and easy allover design, or spend more time on custom, intricate quilting. There's no wrong answer, just lots of options.

These are my favorite tried-and-true techniques that I use in every quilt I make. Once you learn how to break down the quilt-making process into simpler, more manageable tasks, you'll be empowered to make more quilts and enjoy success at every step!

Tools

I have several favorite tools of the trade, but really, the most important tool you'll need in your tool box is a "can-do" attitude.

CUTTING TOOLS

Large Rotary Mat

Get the largest mat you have room for. I do most of my cutting on a rotary cutting mat that measures 24″ × 36″. I have two of these that I place side by side on my cutting counter. This allows me to cut longer lengths for borders and backings.

TIP I also use a small "mini" mat that I keep near my machine for smaller cuts and trimming binding ends.

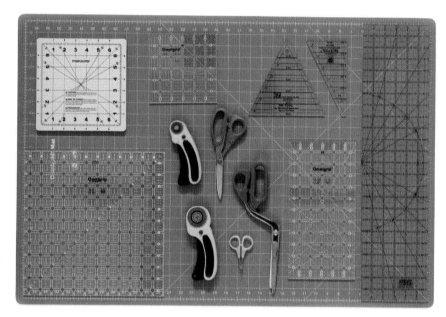

45mm Rotary Cutter with Fresh Blade

The standard size rotary cutter for quilt-making is 45 millimeters and it can easily cut through 4–6 layers of fabric if the blade is nice and sharp. A good rule of thumb is to replace the blade when it feels like you have to apply more pressure to the cutter, or if you feel any nicks or bumps when cutting. There are a variety of cutters; many are ergonomic and can be adjusted for right- or left-handed use. The best way to choose one for yourself is to test a variety of brands and see which feels most comfortable in your hand.

Acrylic Rotary Cutting Rulers

You will need a few! There are three "must-have" sizes that I use on every quilt: a long 6″ × 24″ ruler, a shorter 6″ × 12″ ruler, and a 12½″ × 12½″ or larger square. I mainly use the long ruler for cutting fabric strips and borders. I use the shorter ruler for sub-cutting strips into shorter lengths. I use the square ruler for squaring up the corners of the quilt after it's been quilted. I also have a variety of other sizes that are useful for cutting smaller pieces or specialty shapes. In fact, one of my favorites is a set of Tri-Recs Tools, which I use to make triangle-in-a-square blocks, found in the Daisy Chain pattern (page 72).

I provide two template patterns, the Center Triangle template and the Triangle Pairs template, both used to make the Daisy Chain pattern, so you can make your own cutting guides (see Template Plastic, page 11). They are found in the Appendix (page 126).

Template Plastic

I use template plastic to cut out odd-shaped pieces for which I don't have a specialty ruler. You can also use it to create your own specialty rulers. Simply draw the needed shape onto the template plastic and cut it out with sharp scissors. If all the template edges are straight, you can place a straight acrylic ruler on top of the template to rotary cut each piece of fabric.

Scissors

It's good to have a variety of both fabric and utility scissors for cutting paper or template plastic. I also keep a pair of small thread snips next to my sewing machine at all times for trimming stray threads. Another of my favorite pair of scissors is a very large specialty pair called batting shears. As the name implies, these are specifically for cutting through thick pieces of batting. I can't live without them!

MARKING TOOLS

I rarely mark my quilts, but when I do, it's mainly for straight line quilting, or marking guidelines for walking-foot quilting designs. I have a few favorite marking tools.

>> **Painters tape**   This low tack tape doesn't leave residue on your fabric. Position it exactly where you want the line of quilting to go and stitch right next to the edge of the tape on one or both sides. Be careful not to accidentally stitch on top of the tape. You can also position the edge of the presser foot next to the edge of the tape, so the stitching line is the distance between the edge of the foot and the needle. This is helpful when quilting decorative stitches, or any design where the needle might shift positions.

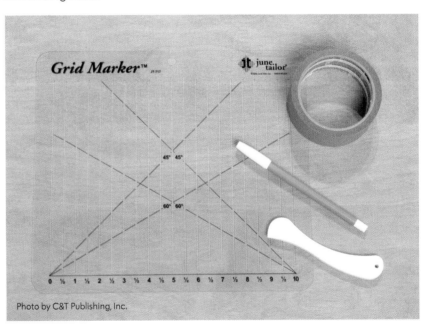

Photo by C&T Publishing, Inc.

>> **Water soluble (blue ink) or air erase (purple ink) marking pen**   These pens mark temporary lines on contrasting fabrics and they either wash out or disappear over time. Just be sure to test them first on scraps to make sure they make a visible line that completely disappears after washing.

>> **Crease Marker**   This plastic tool works great in combination with a straight edge (such as an acrylic ruler or plastic grid marker) for marking straight creases on your fabric. Rather than marking the whole quilt, I usually mark one line at a time, just before I quilt it.

IRON

I prefer to use a hot, dry iron with no steam. Steam can distort fabric or batting, and it can also burn your fingers, especially if you prefer to press your seams open like I do. Also, depending on the hardness of your water, it can cause an iron to spit, or leak dirt on your work. So, play it safe and stick with a dry iron for pressing. If you need to moisten your fabric with water, use a spray bottle with a fine mist, or starch your fabric (page 17).

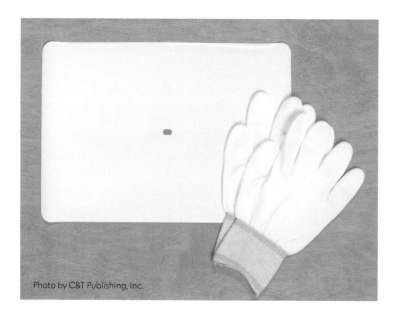

Photo by C&T Publishing, Inc.

GET GRIPPY & SLIPPERY!

Specialty quilting gloves give you the extra grip you need when scrunching and smooshing the quilt through the harp (throat space) of your domestic machine. I prefer gloves that are easy to take on and off, and those with grips in the fingertips that help you grab on to the quilt. Some quilters prefer to have the fingertips cut off to make tasks like threading the needle easier. There are a variety of styles out there; try a few different brands until you find one you like.

A specialty Teflon sheet can be added to the bed of your machine to make the surface slick and slippery, which helps the quilt glide more easily through the machine. I usually only use it for free-motion quilting. If you use it for walking-foot quilting, you'll need to cut out a larger hole near the presser foot area; otherwise, you can inadvertently stitch through the plastic material.

BERNINA 770QE, my machine of choice

SEWING MACHINE

If you don't already have a sewing machine, or are considering buying a new one, choose a machine with the largest throat space that you can afford. Throat space, also called "harp space" is the distance from the needle to the inner right edge of the sewing machine. I recommend at least 7″–10″ of space. This will give you plenty of room to move your quilt with less strain on your body while you quilt.

A few other useful features include needle up/down; presser foot pressure adjustment; extra large bobbins; integrated dual feed; the ability to lower the feed dogs; and the hover feature, which allows you to set the machine foot to automatically lift up slightly when you stop stitching. You can quilt on any sewing machine; the extra bells and whistles just make the job easier.

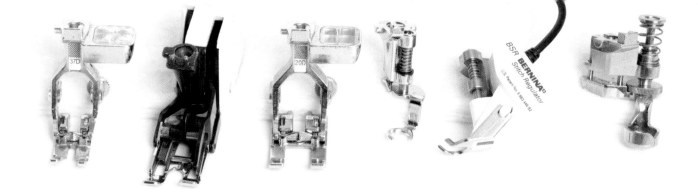

Presser Feet

These are the sewing feet I use to piece and quilt on my home machine.

» **A quarter-inch patchwork foot**   This foot helps stitch perfect ¼″ seams every time. I also use it to apply binding to my quilts. The foot ensures even binding on both sides of the quilt, when I use 2″ wide strips.

» **An open toe walking foot or open toe dual feed foot**   The walking foot may limit how big or wide of a decorative stitch your machine can make, but it pulls all of the layers of the quilt through evenly, eliminating puckers or tucks. An open toe dual feed embroidery foot allows you to see your stitching for straight line quilting, and it allows you to move the needle position for decorative stitching applications. Check your manual for instructions on attaching a guide bar to your foot to quilt lines further apart.

» **An open toe free-motion foot**   Get a foot specifically made to fit your machine. It may look like a circle or an oval. A foot with an "open" toe allows you to see better while quilting. Some machines include a stitch regulator which provides a more consistent stitch length while quilting. A newer specialty foot called an "adjustable ruler-work" foot allows you to quilt with thick machine quilting rulers made especially for this technique.

Needles

Keep plenty of extra needles in your toolbox as you never know when one might break. It's important to match the needle size with the thread weight (see Thread Thoughts, page 18). My preferred thread size is 50 weight cotton; for this thread I recommend using a sharp or topstitch needle, size 80/12. If you prefer a thicker thread (40 weight) then I recommend a larger size needle (size 90/14). For a thinner thread (60 weight), use a smaller needle, such as 70/10.

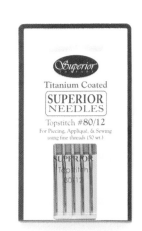

It's also important that the needle have a very pointy point so it cleanly penetrates the layers with each stitch. I advise against using a "universal" needle as it has a more rounded head and does not make as good of a stitch. Sharp and topstitch needles are more suitable. If you like to quilt with specialty threads (such as metallic or clear thread), use a "metallica" needle that has a bigger eye to help prevent thread breakage.

You can also try specialty "machine quilting" needles, but these are usually more expensive, and I haven't seen a difference in stitch quality. My favorite needles are Superior Topstitch titanium-coated needles, and I use them for both piecing and quilting.

Typically, you should change your needle about every 8–12 hours of sewing. However, since most quilters rarely time themselves while sewing, a better gauge is to start with a fresh needle whenever you begin a new sewing project; replace it with a fresh needle once your quilt top is finished and you are ready to begin machine quilting. If you hear a loud thump or click while you sew, or you can tell that your needle is bent, change it right away to prevent damage to your quilt, and for better stitch quality.

Sewing Table

I recommend finding a large sewing table or a cabinet with an opening that drops down, allowing your sewing machine to sit flush with the height of the table. This gives you an additional work surface and more room to maneuver the quilt while machine quilting.

A cabinet or table with an extra leaf off to the left provides more room to hold the weight of the quilt. Extra room on the right of the table is nice to hold notions, such as pins and scissors that you want accessible while quilting.

I recently invented an accessory called "Christa's Quilt Blocks," which attach to the back or side of any table. These are like guardrails for your quilt, ensuring it won't slide off the edge of the table while machine quilting.

If you don't have access to a large sewing table, I recommend getting a portable machine bed extension that slides onto your machine to provide more work surface.

Christa Sewing Cabinet, designed in partnership with Arrow Sewing

Fabric, Thread & Batting

Machine quilting success begins with high-quality materials. They'll last longer, so with proper care, your hand-made treasures can be enjoyed by future generations, too!

FABRIC

I recommend busy, colorful fabrics for two reasons: they add a sense of movement when cut into smaller pieces, and they are great for hiding machine quilting mistakes. By focusing on the overall design of your quilt rather than the individual quilting motifs, you'll enjoy the process and will finish a lot faster, too!

I also like to use colorful, busy prints for the backs of my quilts. This makes it super easy to choose thread colors for machine quilting, and a busy back is great for hiding less-than-perfect stitch tension. Occasionally I'll use scraps from the front of the quilt to create a secondary composition on the back; it's a great way to use up lots of leftover fabrics.

Black, White, and Bright
by Christa Watson for Benartex

Photo by Christa Watson

For best results, choose premium quality, 100% cotton fabrics for your quilts. It can be tempting to skimp on the fabric and purchase inexpensive materials; however, lesser quality fabrics won't hold up as well in the long run. You put so much time and effort into a quilt, you want to make sure your handiwork lasts a lifetime and beyond.

Fabric selvages • Photo by Christa Watson

Standard quilting fabric is approximately 42″ wide from selvage to selvage (the edges of the fabric running along the lengthwise grain), but the usable area is closer to 40″ so that's the number I use to calculate how much fabric I need for a quilt.

You can check the bolt end for fiber content. Premium quality quilting cottons will have a selvage usually with the designer and/or brand name of the fabric purchased. When you find a designer or manufacturer you like, stick with them for consistent quality.

To Prewash or Not to Prewash?

Whether or not to prewash your fabric is a personal preference. I prefer to prewash and starch my fabrics when dealing with yardage or any piece of fabric that is a fat quarter (approximately 18″ × 22″) or larger in size.

Place fat quarter–size pieces in a small mesh garment bag to wash, in order to keep the tangles under control. I throw a few dye-magnet sheets (such as Shout Color Catcher) into each batch of fabric I'm washing, and they'll grab onto any excess dye in the water.

When working with precuts (squares, strips, etc.) I don't prewash. But I do make sure to add several Color Catchers when I wash the finished quilt.

Color Catchers are found in grocery laundry aisle.

TIP I tend to spray starch uncut fabric rather than finished, pieced blocks, and I only starch the amount of washed fabric I plan to use.

To starch fabric, spray one side of the fabric and let it rest for a few minutes; then flip the fabric over and iron it from the opposite side. Then spray the newly ironed side and flip the fabric over to starch from the other side again. This allows the starch to penetrate the cloth and prevents the starch from burning and flaking off on the iron.

THREAD THOUGHTS

Thread size is based on thread thickness and how much a certain length of thread weighs. For instance, size 40-weight thread is generally thicker than size 50-weight; size 30-weight is thicker than 40-weight, and so on.

However, because thread types vary, and the numbering system isn't applied uniformly, one brand's 50 weight may be completely different from another brand. My recommendation is to try different brands, fibers, and weights until you find one (or more) that you like.

TIP Spools of thread are either cross wound in a zig-zag pattern where it looks like there's an 'x' across the spool of thread or stacked, where the thread is wound parallel to the spool without crossing itself. Cross wound thread should be positioned horizontally on your machine; stacked thread should be positioned vertically. I use a separate thread stand, which can accommodate either type of spool as well as larger cones of thread. This puts more distance between the thread and the machine which aids in smoother thread delivery. Smoother thread leads to better stitch quality, which is what we are aiming for in our quilts.

My favorite thread is Aurifil 50-weight 100% cotton thread. It's thin, yet strong, and because it's a natural fiber, it sinks into your quilt, providing good stitch definition. I use it for everything: piecing, quilting, appliqué, binding, and even a little garment sewing. Cotton thread washes and shrinks at the same rate as the cotton fabrics you use, so they'll naturally wear at the same rate.

Rather than getting confused trying to remember which thread weight and type to use for different applications, I like to simplify things by choosing *one* thread type and stocking up on as many different colors as I can.

Christa's thread collections
with Aurifil: 50-weight 100% cotton

Auditioning thread colors

Choosing Thread Colors

For piecing my quilt blocks and tops, I like to use a neutral-colored thread, or one that seems to blend in with most of the fabric colors. I don't worry about changing thread colors while piecing, but I tend to piece with a variety of grays, tans, and pastel-colored threads.

TIP If you always use 100% cotton thread for machine quilting, leftover bobbins can be used to piece your next scrappy quilt!

When it comes to choosing thread colors for machine quilting, I prefer for my thread to blend in with my quilt top. This is another way to hide perfectly imperfect quilting so that all you see is gorgeous quilting texture. To determine which thread blends the best, audition your choices by pulling out about 8″–10″ of thread from 2–3 different spools you are considering. Lay them on top of the quilt top so they span several different fabric colors. Notice which thread seems to disappear the most and choose that one for machine quilting.

I also recommend using the same color thread in the top and bobbin. If you use a highly contrasting thread combination such as white thread in the top and black thread in the bobbin (or vice versa) you may end up with what I call "pokies"—little dots of black or white on either side of your quilt. Adjusting the tension can help, but it's hard to get it perfectly balanced. To make things easier, stick with the same color thread in the top and in the bobbin to camouflage any tension issues.

If you are concerned that you don't have enough thread for both the needle and bobbin, then choose two colors that are similar in value. For example, if I'm quilting with a light yellow colored top thread, I might use a slightly different shade of yellow for the bobbin, or a similar value thread such as a light green in the bobbin. When in doubt, choose a thread color that is slightly lighter than the fabrics in your quilt. A lighter thread quilted on darker fabric looks much better than a darker thread quilted on a lighter fabric.

Which do you like best? Dark thread on light fabric, or light thread on dark fabric?

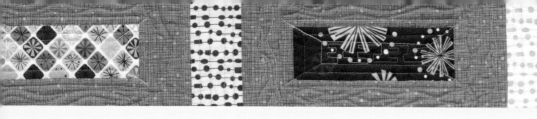

Adjusting Thread Tension

Think of stitch tension as a tug of war. If the top or bobbin thread is pulling too hard, one of them will "win" the tug-of-war. For example, if your top tension is too tight, it will pull the bobbin thread up to the top. If the bobbin tension is too tight, it will pull the top thread to the back of the quilt. To adjust the tension, the winning side needs to loosen up (decrease) the amount of tension. Or the "losing" side needs to increase its tension. See the operating manual for your machine for more information on making tension adjustments.

It's best to adjust the machine tension for the top thread only. There should be a knob or dial on your machine that allows you to increase or decrease the top thread tension. To find the best tension for your project, make an adjustment and then practice stitching on a small swatch of the project fabric. Repeat until the stitch tension is correct.

If you feel you need to adjust the bobbin tension and you have a removable bobbin case, I recommend purchasing a second bobbin case for machine quilting. Only ever adjust the second bobbin case, following your manufacturer's instructions for adjusting the bobbin tension.

If you have a removable bobbin case, you can do a bobbin tension test to determine if the bottom thread is the problem. Insert the bobbin into the case and grasp the thread while you give it a little yank, sort of like letting a yo-yo fall from its string. Good bobbin tension should allow the bobbin to fall down slightly without letting go of all the thread.

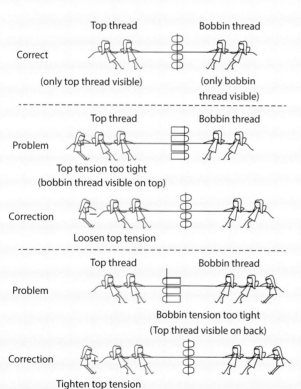

Correct — Top thread / Bobbin thread
(only top thread visible) (only bobbin thread visible)

Problem — Top thread / Bobbin thread
Top tension too tight (bobbin thread visible on top)

Correction — Loosen top tension

Problem — Top thread / Bobbin thread
Bobbin tension too tight (Top thread visible on back)

Correction — Tighten top tension

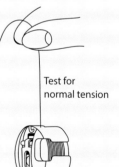

Test for normal tension

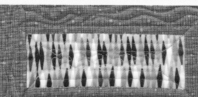

BATTING

Contrary to popular belief, quilting densely on your quilt will *not* make it stiff, as long as you use natural fiber materials. By this, I mean 100% cotton fabrics (mentioned earlier), 100% cotton thread (my favorite), and natural fiber batting such as cotton, wool, silk or bamboo. Making your quilt entirely from natural materials allows it to breathe, and the more you wash your quilt, the softer and cuddlier it will be!

My favorite natural fiber battings are cotton and wool. Cotton batting drapes nicely within your quilt. It lies flat and shrinks when you wash it, giving that antique puckery look, which is great for hiding any quilting irregularities. Cotton batting also clings to your fabric, which helps to prevent puckers and tucks while machine quilting. The only downside of cotton is that it has a memory, which means it will show fold lines and creases. It's also denser and heavier than other battings.

Wool batting is light and fluffy and gives more stitch definition to your quilting. It doesn't have the same memory as cotton, so fold lines and creases are not

Photo by C&T Publishing, Inc.

as prominent. Wool is a great choice for quilts that are refolded often, sent through the mail, or hung in a quilt show because the fold lines don't show. The downside of wool is that some people are allergic to it, and depending on the brand, it might smell like wet sheep when damp!

My absolute favorite batting is a combination of 80% cotton and 20% wool (Hobbs Tuscany Cotton Wool Batting) because it combines the best of both worlds. I recommend trying a variety of battings on the next several quilts you make. Take a picture of the batting package with your quilt top so you remember which type you used. Then make notes on how it feels while quilting, how much it shrinks, and how you like the overall appearance of the quilt when finished. If you can settle on one or two favorites, that's one less decision you'll need to make for future quilts!

TIP Unroll the batting from the package and allow it to "rest" for a few days to reduce any wrinkles. You can also relax wrinkles by throwing the batting in a dryer with a wet towel for a few minutes or by pressing the batting with a hot dry iron. (For delicate batting, use a piece of fabric to cover it while you press.)

Preparing the Quilt

Preparing your quilt for machine quilting is like prepping the inside of your home for painting; painting the walls isn't difficult, but all the prep work of moving the furniture and taping around the windows can be a bit tedious. The same thing applies to getting your quilt ready for machine quilting. Taking the time to do this important step allows you to enjoy the machine quilting process and achieve much better results.

CUTTING AND PIECING

Fundamental to successful quilting is accurate measuring, careful cutting, and straight stitching with a uniform seam allowance width.

Cutting

Measure twice and cut once to avoid cutting mistakes, then take the time to make good, accurate cuts.

To cut through multiple fabric layers, fold the fabric so the selvage edges roughly align and hold the fabric in front of you with the fabric fold at the bottom. Look for any warping or skewing of the fabric; if you see any, use your fingers to adjust the selvages to the left or right so that the folded fabric hangs straight. Once the fabric hangs straight, lay the folded side along one of the horizontal lines on the cutting mat.

Make fabric cuts perpendicular to the fabric fold, using the vertical lines on the ruler and mat as a guide for accuracy. Make sure there is always fabric underneath the ruler as you cut.

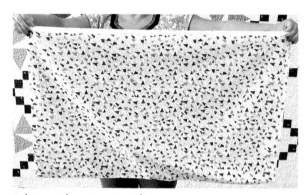

Fabric not hanging straight

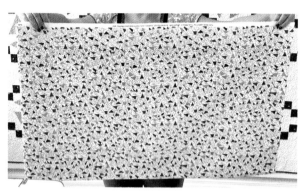

Fabric hanging straight • Photos by Christa Watson

TIP If the ruler slips while you are cutting, you might find that cut pieces are slightly off the correct size making it difficult to sew them together. Get non-slip rulers, or place sandpaper, or specialty non-slip dots, underneath the rulers while cutting to prevent slipping.

Piecing

It is essential to stitch pieces together with an accurate ¼″ seam. If your units are just slightly off, that mistake can magnify itself over an entire block or quilt top.

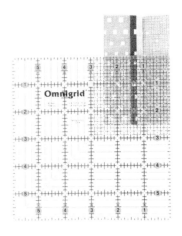

It is a good idea to stitch a test seam to ensure accuracy.

1. Cut 2 fabric rectangles, each 1½″ by 4″ and sew them with right sides together.

2. Press the seam open and measure the width of the piece. It should be exactly 2½″ wide.

3. If it's not, adjust your seam allowance until you get the correct measurement.

TIPS FOR ACCURATE PIECING

» Always sew the entire seam and don't veer off at the ends of your units. Slow down if needed and use a stiletto to keep your pieces together while sewing.

» The best way to prevent thread jams or uneven stitches is to avoid putting lumps and bumps in your quilts. Therefore, I recommend pressing *all* seams open throughout your quilt. Not only will it be easier to join the seams, but your blocks and quilt top will lie very flat. Contrary to popular belief, you CAN stitch in the ditch with seams pressed open. In fact, it secures your quilt and gives added strength to your seams.

» To ensure that your seams don't split open while handling, reduce your stitch length while piecing. For example, the default stitch length on my machine is 2.5mm per stitch. I turn the stitch length down to 2.0mm which makes for a nice, tight seam. It also helps ensure that whatever thread I use for piecing won't show through the seams. Sewing with a shorter stitch length also strengthens each seam since there is more thread holding it together. The only downside is that shorter stitches make it harder to do the "frog" stitch—the one that goes, "Rip-it! Rip-it! Rip-it!"

» I also recommend making a test block from scrap fabrics before sewing the whole quilt top. This helps you follow the pattern directions to understand how the units are constructed. Once you are comfortable with the step-by-step process, I recommend assembly line sewing, also known as "chain" piecing.

TIP / **Sew all the units for the same block at the same time with right sides together. Rather than clipping the threads after each sewn unit and starting fresh, sew a few stitches in between each pair of units to sew. This fast process allows you to sew almost continuously while making the quilt top or blocks.**

» Begin and end each sewing session with a scrap piece of fabric called a "leader" or "ender" depending on whether that fabric scrap is at the beginning or end of your pieced chain. Using this piece of scrap fabric to catch your starting and ending thread tails keeps the process neat and tidy.

The "leader" begins a session of chain piecing.

BACKING

The easiest way to back your quilt is to use extra-wide fabric that is larger than your quilt top. However, the fabric options are limited, so I usually sew 2 or more pieces of fabric together to get the size that I need.

To figure out how much fabric you'll need to sew a backing made from regular quilting yardage, add 12″ to the length and width of the finished quilt top. This gives you approximately 6″ all around all 4 sides. The extra fabric will make it much easier when it's time to baste your quilt, so you don't have to line everything up perfectly (see Basting, page 26).

For example, the *Loose Weave* quilt (page 90) finishes at 59″ × 71″, so you should plan on the backing measuring approximately 71″ × 83″. For this sized quilt, you can sew a backing using 2 lengths of 40″–44″-wide fabric that are each 2½ yards long. When you join them parallel to the selvage, the seamed fabric is approximately 80″ × 90″, which is more than large enough for the backing.

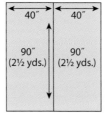

Pieced quilt backing from two lengths of the same fabric

However, for a larger quilt such as Daisy Chain (page 72), you'll need 3 lengths of 40″–44″-wide fabric with 2 seams sewn parallel to the selvages. The finished quilt top is 90″ × 90″, which means you want a backing piece that measures approximately 102″ × 102″. Conveniently, 3 yards of fabric measures 108″ × 40″. So, if you purchase 3 pieces of 3 yards each (9 yards total), the finished backing is approximately 108″ × 120″ once it's sewn together. Again, this is more than enough. As you get comfortable with the basting and quilting process, you may be able to get away with less fabric, but this is a good way to start.

If my backing is made from many different fabrics, I'll sew using ¼″ seams. If it is made from 2–3 long lengths of fabric, I'll trim the selvages and sew with ½″ seams.

Pieced quilt backing from three lengths of fabric; they can be same or different.

Make a Pieced Backing

For an added touch of customization, you can make a pieced backing from scraps, or random pieces of leftover yardage. I like to use up discarded pieces from the front and I enjoy combining them with fabrics in a similar color family. In fact, I sort my leftover scraps by color so that at any time I can sew them together into larger, improvisationally pieced units.

My favorite way to make a scrappy backing is what I call the "puzzle" method. Simply place your finished quilt top on a design wall or other flat surface and cover it with sections of pieced fabric until it's completely covered with about 4″ to 6″ of fabric sticking out beyond the pieced quilt top on all 4 sides.

This is the technique I used for the back of the red and pink Loose Weave quilt, using leftover fabrics in similar colors from other quilts. I created 5 pieced panels to cover the quilt top as shown on page 25.

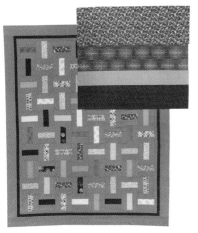

First panel section
covering upper right.

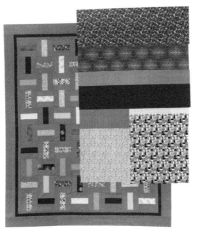

Second panel section below right,
trimmed and joined to first.

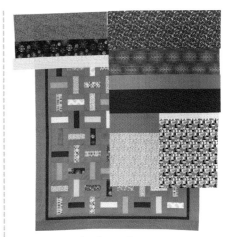

Third panel section
placed upper left.

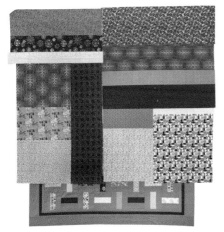

Fourth panel section placed
lower left, sewn to third panel.

Panels 1–4 joined; fifth panel section
sewn across the entire bottom
edge of quilt top.

There's not much math involved with sewing a scrappy pieced backing. You basically build it piece-by-piece, creating sections. Every pieced backing is unique! Make sure each piece overlaps as you lay them out. Then "puzzle" it together by sewing 2 pieces at a time, trimming each piece to fit as you go. Sew smaller scraps and strips into square- or rectangle units. Then sew those units together into vertical or horizontal panels.

Join smaller panel sections to larger ones, trimming the units to fit as needed. Continue adding panel sections until the entire quilt top is covered. Use leftover precut strips to fill in the gaps where sections aren't quite the same size. For best results, ensure that the outer edges of the pieced quilt back are made from larger pieces of fabric. There's no need to make the outer edges around the quilt even as the extra will get trimmed away later. It takes longer to make this type of improvisational backing, but it will definitely make a statement!

BASTING

One of the secrets to successful machine quilting is basting your quilts properly. I used to safety-pin baste until I discovered spray basting, which is quicker and more efficient.

My favorite method uses specially formulated adhesive spray (I prefer the 505 brand) and my design wall. (See my step-by-step tutorial on building a design wall at my website; for the link, see About the Author, page 127.) You can modify this technique and baste your quilts on a table, but I prefer the design wall because I can get up close to the quilt to ensure it stays nice and flat. I spray the quilt layers together outside, and then bring them inside to assemble.

TIP / **If you prefer to pin baste, smooth out the quilt layers one at a time on a large table; then use lots of safety pins to secure. Place the safety pins about 2″ apart all throughout the quilt. Make sure you remove the pins as you quilt so you don't accidentally stitch over them.**

How to Spray Baste

You will need spray adhesive, a large sheet, outdoor table (or flat ground), acrylic ruler, design wall and straight pins (or large table), and batting scissors.

1. Press the quilt top and backing and clip any stray threads.

2. Remove the batting from the package or unroll as needed. If you have a large roll of batting, roughly determine how much you need by pulling it across the width of the quilt top then roughly cut so it extends several inches past the quilt top edge on both sides. The batting is folded in half so there will be plenty for the length of the quilt, too. I save any

excess trimmed batting for making practice quilt samples.

My favorite batting is Hobbs Tuscany Cotton/Wool by the roll. • Photo by Susanne Shultis

3. Measure or trim the batting to ensure that it is at least 4″ larger around all four sides of the quilt top. Measure the backing piece to ensure that it is at least 6″ larger than the quilt top on all four sides.

TIP / **An easy way to ensure that the batting and backing are large enough is to lay out your finished quilt top on them. Make sure there is a sufficient amount of the backing and batting sticking out beyond all four sides of the quilt top.**

4. It is best to spray baste outside so that the fumes can dissipate, but you can do it inside in a well-ventilated room if you wear a protective face mask. If needed, lay a sheet on the ground or a table to protect your quilt and catch any over-spray. Shake the can of adhesive and spray a few squirts away from the quilt to ensure that the nozzle is clean and the spray comes out evenly before you start.

5. Lay the quilt backing—wrong side up—on a sheet on the ground or table outside and apply a thin coat of spray adhesive evenly across the surface of the quilt backing. Walk around the quilt backing as needed to reach all areas of the quilt. Fold the backing, sticky side out, and set it aside so you can spray the quilt top.

6. Repeat the process for the quilt top, using the design of the quilt to help you keep track of which areas you've already covered with spray. Don't worry if the quilt top and backing have some give or are a bit wrinkly from movement. You will smooth them both out later.

Spraying the quilt backing

Spraying the quilt top

7. Once the backing and quilt top are sprayed, it's okay to fold them up, sticky side out, and bring them inside to assemble the layers together on a design wall, table, or other flat surface. The layers will be tacky to the touch, but you can easily unfold the layers and peel them apart. If you can, complete the basting process on the same day to prevent the spray from drying out. However, you can wait several weeks before quilting if needed; the adhesive won't separate once the quilt has been basted.

Quilt top and backing have both been sprayed with adhesive and are ready to assemble.

8. Pin the quilt backing, wrong side up, to the top of the design wall. (Mine is made from foam insulation board covered with a white flannel sheet). Let gravity pull the weight of the fabric down. Gently pull apart any of the fabric sticking to itself and spend some time smoothing it all out with your hands or a long acrylic ruler. I have an extra ruler that I use exclusively for this purpose.

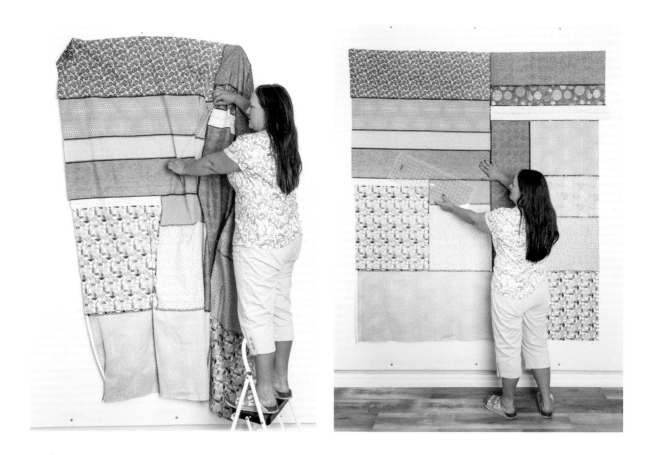

TIP Your hands and the ruler will get a bit sticky, but the residue easily washes off with soap and water. Spend as much time as you need to straighten the backing so that it's nice and smooth and flat on the design wall.

9. Next, place the batting on top of the backing. Ideally, the backing should extend around all 4 sides of the backing. However, in the image below you can see that the batting sticks out a little on one side and that's ok! Don't worry about lining the batting up perfectly; the extra fabric around all four sides provides some wiggle room. The batting is trimmed later, so it's okay if it's not perfectly straight. Smooth it out with your hands or a long acrylic ruler.

10. Place the quilt top in the same manner, over the batting and the backing, so the right side of the quilt faces out. Pin generously along the top edge and let gravity pull on the weight of the quilt top so it hangs straight. Ensure that there is extra batting and backing sticking out around all four sides of the quilt top.

11. Continue smoothing out the top layer once it's on the wall. Use the acrylic ruler to help you work out any bubbles and ensure that the seam lines are nice and straight. Once your basted quilt is flat, smooth and straight, machine quilting it will be a breeze!

12. Trim some, but not all the excess batting and backing away from the quilt top. I prefer to leave only about an inch or two around all four sides so that the excess doesn't flip itself under the quilt while quilting.

TIP I use specialty batting shears to cut my batting and trim the layers while basting. They are much easier to use than regular scissors and they cut through multiple thick layers easily!

13. With a hot dry iron, press both sides of the spray basted quilt to set the glue. This ensures that all three layers stay together without shifting and eliminates the need for pins. You can still pull apart the layers if you need to adjust the top, batting or backing.

This also provides a final chance to press out any wrinkles and work out any fullness in the quilt. I prefer to iron the back side of the quilt first, and then flip it over to the front side. I'm using a big extension board on top of my ironing board (known as a "Big Board"). This provides more surface area, making the job easier.

Note You can repeat this process on a table if you don't have a large flat surface or a design wall. When smoothing out each layer, work the center section that's on the table first. Then pull the quilt to one side or the other until you've smoothed out each layer of the entire quilt. Iron the basted quilt as mentioned above and you are ready to quilt!

Practice, Practice, Practice!

In order to successfully machine quilt, you need to have a go-to set of designs that you enjoy stitching and that you can easily accomplish without frustration. The best way to achieve results that make you happy is by first sketching out the designs on paper so you can get a feel for the flow of the design and how to form various quilting motifs. Once you feel comfortable drawing motifs, practice stitching them on small quilt samples before quilting them on a full-sized quilt. Think of it this way—if you can sketch it, you can stitch it!

The following pages demonstrate two quilting techniques: walking-foot *or* free-motion quilting. Before starting to sketch, refer to the gallery of walking-foot quilting designs (page 40) and the gallery of free-motion quilting designs (page 50) for inspiration.

SKETCH IT

To understand how any of the designs in this book are formed, first trace it with your finger, from start to finish. Then pick a design to draw over and over on a piece of paper until it feels natural and comfortable. You aren't trying to draw an exact duplicate of what is shown, but instead your interpretation of the design.

What are some of your favorite motifs to stitch? Don't forget—inspiration is all around you. Look at other quilts that you like for more ideas; or sit and doodle every day to see what other ideas you come up with. Take notice of shapes in architecture and nature, too. If you can doodle an unbroken line over and over, chances are it will make a great quilting motif!

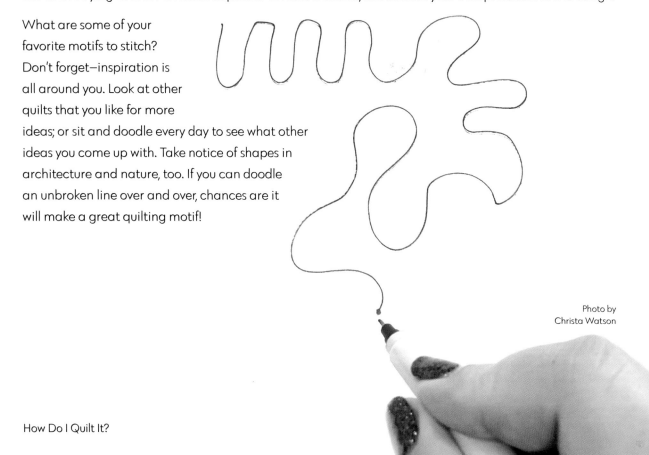

Photo by Christa Watson

PREPARE A PRACTICE SAMPLE

Create a practice quilting sample using 2 squares of 100% cotton fabric 8″ or larger, with a square of batting in between. If you would like to mimic the feel of a basted quilt, make the batting and bottom square slightly larger than the top square. Try to use fabrics that are like your pieced quilt top. You might want to make an actual pieced block for your sample, to practice quilting with seams. Or you can use leftovers and scraps to make various sized samples to practice on. Use the same type of thread and batting that you plan to use in your quilt so you can see how all the materials interact with each other.

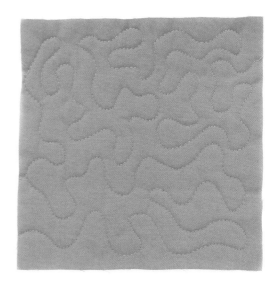

You don't need to baste the layers for a small practice sample, also known as a "quilt sandwich." The fabrics should cling to the batting well enough to hold it together while practicing.

As you practice, take note of things you like or don't like, such as how well the thread glides through the sample, or how much texture or stitch definition you can see in each piece. I also recommend trying out several different battings to see which type you like best.

STITCHING GUIDELINES

Whenever possible, I prefer to quilt with a continuous line whether I'm stitching with a walking foot or free-motion quilting. I try to plan my quilting to start "off the quilt" in the batting at the top or side of the quilt; then end the stitching in the batting on the bottom or other side of the quilt (see Make a Quilting Plan, page 63). In this way, all the starts, stops, and messy thread tails get trimmed away once I square up the quilt for finishing, and the edges of the quilting are covered by the binding.

However, there may be occasions where I need to start a quilting design away from the quilt edges, such as if I run out of thread or break a needle; or if the design motif starts and ends in a particular location on the quilt. If possible, I try to hide the starts and stops in a seam to make them less noticeable.

TIP Always thread your machine with the presser foot raised. This opens the tension discs so that the machine can be threaded properly.

Begin Stitching

To begin stitching, pull the bobbin thread up through the thread plate by inserting the needle down into the quilt sandwich, lowering the presser foot, and then raising the needle and foot up again. Basically, what you've done is taken one stitch in place. Grasp both the top and bobbin thread with your hand and pull both threads underneath and away from the presser foot. If it helps, use a pin or needle to pull the end of the bobbin thread loose.

TIP / **Follow this sequence to pull up the bobbin thread: needle down, foot down; needle up, foot up.**

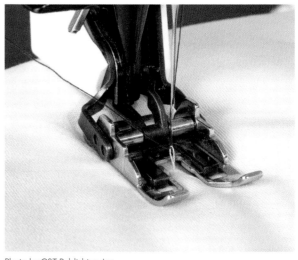

Photo by C&T Publishing, Inc.

Secure the Stitches

If you aren't starting at the edge of the quilt, you need to secure the stitches at the beginning and end of stitching.

THE UTILITARIAN METHOD

Starting: Lower the presser foot and insert the needle in your quilt. While gently holding the excess thread tails with your left hand, take 6–8 teeny tiny stitches forward to lock them in place. Your stitches should move forward no more than about ⅛˝.

Stopping: When you've reached the end of your line of quilting, either reduce your stitch length, or hold your quilt slightly in place to make another series of 6–8 tiny stitches, stopping right where you want the stitching line to finish. These teeny tiny stitches will be very difficult to remove, and they should not be stacked on top of each other like a knot. Clip the excess thread tails once the stitches are secure.

TIP / **If you run out of bobbin thread or break a needle in the middle of a design, reload the bobbin or replace the needle. Then back up about ½˝, pull the bobbin thread to the top again, and stitch 6–8 teeny tiny stitches on top of the previous line of stitching to secure it. Continue stitching to complete the design. If you use a thin thread like cotton, this will be less noticeable.**

THE TYING OFF METHOD

Starting: Rather than quilting tiny starting stitches, pull the bobbin thread up to the top. Then begin stitching your motif at a normal stitch length. Quilt for about an inch so that the presser foot is out of the way and so you can easily grab the top and bottom thread tails and tie them into a knot by hand. Keep the knot as close to the surface of the quilt as possible.

Thread both tails into the eye of a hand sewing needle and insert the thread through the quilt at the beginning of the line of stitching. Give the needle a yank to pop the knot into the batting to hide it.

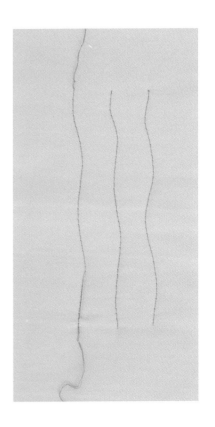

TIP Use a self-threading hand sewing needle, also known as a "cheater" needle to make tying off easier. This type of needle has a slit in the hole that the thread can slip into, making threading much quicker.

Photo by
C&T Publishing, Inc.

Stopping: To bring the bobbin thread up at the end of a line of stitching, manually take one stitch forward, raise the needle and presser foot, and then pull your quilt a few inches away from the machine to create slack in the needle and bobbin threads. Clip the thread from both sides of the quilt, leaving several inches of a thread tail on either side. Use a pin to pull the bobbin thread through to the top. Make a knot by hand and then pop it into the batting as previously instructed.

I don't mind tying off knots a few times in the quilt where smaller stitches would be noticeable, but if there are many stops and starts, this can get tedious very quickly.

Walking-Foot Quilting

I recommend getting comfortable with walking-foot quilting before moving on to free-motion. Walking-foot quilting builds your skills while increasing your confidence, especially when quilting a large quilt.

WALKING-FOOT PRACTICE

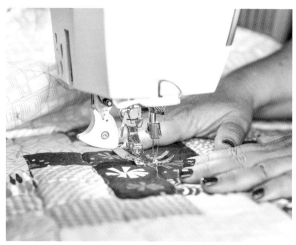

You can use a traditional walking foot, or your sewing machine's built-in dual feed system (if your machine has dual feed). They perform the same function and I refer to the terms interchangeably.

Photo by Susanne Shultis

Walking foot/dual feed quilting is similar to regular straight-line sewing. The feed dogs are up or engaged, just like when you are piecing a quilt. When you press the foot pedal, the feed dogs pull the quilt through the machine in a forward motion.

» Because of the bulk, there tends to be a lot of friction and drag on the quilt during stitching, which tends to shrink up the quilting stitches. To compensate, I usually make my quilting stitches longer than for standard stitching. On my machine, *I turn the stitch length up to 3.0 from its default of 2.5.* This is mainly a matter of personal preference, so try out a few different stitch lengths to see the look you prefer.

» I prefer to quilt long lines of quilting in one direction, rather than going back and forth in opposite directions, which can cause whiskering (wrinkles) and puckers on the quilt. For example, if I'm stitching a series of lines all the way across the quilt, I start quilting at the top of the quilt (in the excess batting that's sticking out) and quilt the full line from the top to the bottom of the quilt (vertically). In other words, I push the quilt away from myself as it feeds through the machine, while the stitches come towards me. *I look directly where I need to make the next stitch, which is just in front of the needle.*

» If I need to quilt horizontal or diagonal lines, I rotate the quilt so that from my perspective, I'm still stitching the quilt in a vertical motion. If the quilt is too bulky to fit under the machine, I quilt half of the lines from top to bottom, then rotate the quilt 180° and stitch the remaining lines in the opposite direction. However, my perspective remains the same because I still move the quilt forward, stitching the lines from top to bottom.

TIP If your machine has the option, lower your presser foot pressure to prevent pleats while walking-foot quilting. This is especially helpful when crossing over a previous line of stitching. On my machine, the default pressure is set to 50; I turn it all the way down to 0. This is not necessary when free-motion quilting because there's less pressure on the quilt to begin with.

Walking-Foot Quilting Designs

Every walking-foot quilting design can be quilted 3 different ways: with straight lines, wavy lines, or with decorative stitches (if your machine has those capabilities). Practice stitching out the designs that follow on a practice sample before trying them out on a real quilt.

QUILTING STRAIGHT LINES

To quilt straight lines, use a zig-zag needle plate (the one with the wider hole) in case you want to change needle position while quilting. Install the walking foot or engage the dual feed system and begin sewing in a forward motion, ensuring that all 3 layers of the quilt move smoothly through the machine.

Use your hands to guide the quilt slowly through the machine, but let the machine do most of the work. Follow the seam, marked line, or quilting plan (see Make a Quilt Plan, page 63) you've chosen for your quilt.

TIP **Increase your stitch length as desired to create the look you prefer.**

>> The most popular straight lines are "in the ditch." That means quilting in the seams between two different fabrics. This can be done with every piecing seam as desired (not my preference), or in certain key areas of the quilt to secure it for additional quilting later. (I call this "anchor" quilting.)

>> Straight lines can also be quilted next to the ditch, using the edge of the presser foot as a guide. The width of the presser foot from the needle to the edge of the foot determines how widely spaced the lines will be. This is called "echo" quilting because you are making an echo of a previous line of quilting. Place the edge of your foot next to the ditch (or a previously stitched line). Quilt a line next to it, following the outline of the previously stitched line.

Quilting straight lines is very straightforward.

>> To quilt a wider or narrower "echo" line, you can mark the line spacing, change the needle position, or use a guide attached to the presser foot.

>> Straight lines can be used to quilt a variety of geometric designs. Whenever it's time to stitch in a different direction, stop with the needle down in the quilt, rotate the quilt and continue stitching. As a rule of thumb, the more the design changes directions, the more often you'll need to rotate the quilt to accomplish the design. Mark the line if desired, or skip the marking and let your lines be more organic and straight-"ish."

Quilting Wavy Lines

Wavy lines are actually much faster and easier to quilt than straight ones. The more you move the quilt, the bigger the waves will be. Enjoy the whimsical nature of this technique and don't try to line up the waves from line to line; the more natural, the better!

To quilt wavy lines, turn the quilt ever so slightly while you stitch. Use your hands to help guide the quilt through the machine. Grasp the sides of the quilt to gently move the quilt back and forth; or use the palms of your hands or your fingertips to gently wiggle the quilt. Each wavy line you quilt will be unique and will add personality to your design!

» Try quilting wavy lines near the ditch or on top of the ditch as opposed to straight lines in the ditch. You can also quilt all sorts of grids in a hurry with wavy lines. And the best part is, they don't need to be marked. You can usually eyeball the distance you want to quilt with wavy lines.

Photo by C&T Publishing, Inc.

Quilting Decorative Stitches

If your machine has decorative stitch capabilities, you can have a lot of fun adding texture to your quilts. After all, you paid for those fancy stitches so you might was well use them! Choose decorative stitches that have a light and airy look to them rather than a very dense and thready design.

To quilt decorative lines, be sure the zigzag plate is installed so that you don't break a needle. Select a decorative stitch on your machine, following the instructions in your owners' manual.

Stitch one line across your practice sample, with the machine set at the default stitch settings. This is your baseline to compare. Then increase the length and width settings as far as your machine will safely allow. Quilt another line next to your first line and make a note of the length and width settings. Next, quilt additional lines of decorative stitches, adjusting the length and width settings as desired.

The best stitch settings are a matter of personal preference. Once you find the look that you like, make a note of the settings right on your practice sample so that you can re-create the pattern on your project. Repeat this process for several more decorative stitches to create a go-to set of designs to quilt!

Adjusting the length and width of the various decorative stitches. • Photo by C&T Publishing, Inc.

TIP One word of caution—check your manual to determine whether you can quilt decorative stitches with your walking foot. Some walking feet do not have enough area in between the legs of the foot to form a decorative stitch; or the size of stitch you can make may be limited. This is one of the reasons I prefer to use the BERNINA dual feed system with an open toe embroidery foot (20D foot). I can quilt the full width of any decorative stitch, which gives me endless possibilities!

Try It!

Quilt each design shown here on a separate practice sample. Stitch slowly until you are comfortable with your movement, then speed up slightly, but stay in control. After all, this is "walking" foot quilting, not running foot quilting!

For more variety, try combining the 3 stitching techniques—straight lines, wavy lines and decorative stitches—in the same design. Just remember—if you can dream it—you can stitch it!

Try straight lines and wavy lines in the same design!

Photos by C&T Publishing, Inc.

Move your quilt to form waves while you quilt with a decorative stitch!

Switch between several different decorative stitches while quilting a larger design for a more artistic effect.

GALLERY OF WALKING-FOOT QUILTING DESIGNS

The following pages provide instructions for basic—and some more intricate—walking-foot quilting designs. I've also included illustrations for a few bonus ideas to try!

To practice any of these designs, draw a square on a plain piece of paper and sketch out your chosen motif. Then quilt it on a plain fabric sample, or a simple pieced block. Use the images and diagrams to guide you as you stitch., but do not try to replicate the stitch path exactly.

Rotate each sample as needed so that you are always stitching each from top to bottom, from your perspective. See the corresponding quilt and page number to see how each design is stitched on an actual quilt.

Whenever the instructions indicate "wavy lines," you can stitch wavy lines or decorative stitches. Remember, you can mix and match these quilting designs. The sky's the limit when it comes to your creativity!

Note The following examples are all stitched with **contrasting thread for visibility. In "real" life quilting, I use more subtle, blending thread to match. Remember, you can stitch the designs more or less densely than shown.**

Radiating Lines

See Floral Spray (page 78).

These straight lines begin at or near the same point and radiate out in one direction, filling in all the available space.

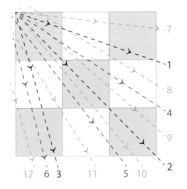

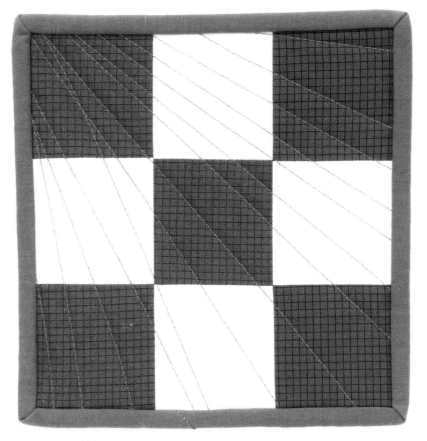

Photo by C&T Publishing, Inc.

To quilt the lines in an organized way, first stitch all the black lines, then the red lines, then the blue lines. Stitch roughly from the corner all the way across to the other side. It's okay if some of the lines overlap at the corner. You can also quilt additional lines in between the numbered lines for increased stitch density.

BONUS IDEAS

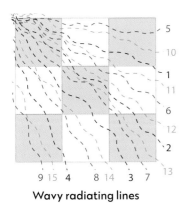

Wavy radiating lines

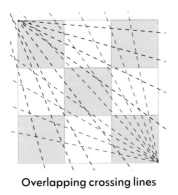

Overlapping crossing lines

TIP The suggested stitching order in these diagrams will allow you to quilt methodically across the piece, spreading out the density of the stitching to avoid puckers. This enables you to anchor or secure each section of the block (or quilt) and fill in with additional quilting as desired.

Stitch in the Ditch

See Angles & Curves (page 118).

Stitch straight lines directly over the patchwork seams. This causes the unquilted areas to pop up. You can stitch some of the seams or all of them. Stitch slowly to stay in the ditch. The stitching might not be very visible, but it will stabilize the quilt.

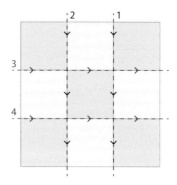

Stitching-in-the-ditch combined with stitching near the ditch

Photo by C&T Publishing, Inc.

Start at the top of the block on the rightmost seam and quilt the line straight down across the sample. Quilt the vertical lines first (black lines). Rotate the sample to quilt the lines in the other direction (red lines).

BONUS IDEAS

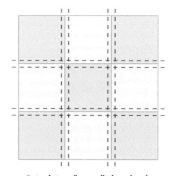

Stitching "near" the ditch

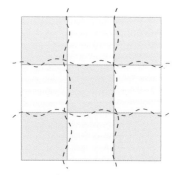

Wavy lines "over" the ditch

Parallel Lines

See Chain Links (page 86).

Stitch a series of straight lines across the sample at any angle, but parallel to each other.

Lines can be stitched in both directions across the quilt, forming a grid where they intersect.

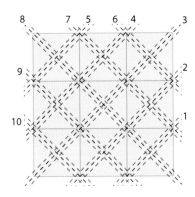

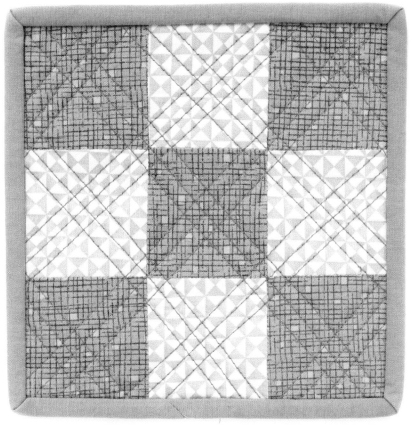

Photo by C&T Publishing, Inc.

Quilt the longest lines first to stabilize the quilt (black lines). Add additional parallel lines as desired (red lines). For additional stability, you may wish to stitch in the ditch along major seamlines before starting this design.

BONUS IDEAS

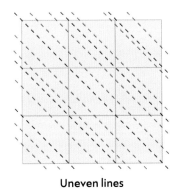

Uneven lines

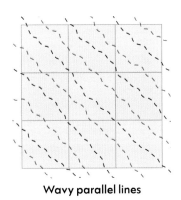

Wavy parallel lines

Random Grid

See Random Crosshatch
(page 94).

Stitching in the ditch is done first
to stabilize the quilt. Then, stitch
additional lines at random intervals until the desired spacing is
achieved. The exact number of
lines may vary.

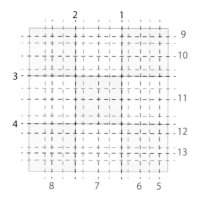

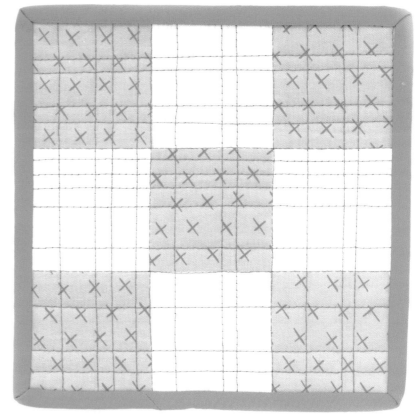

Photo by C&T Publishing, Inc.

Stitch in the ditch along all major horizontal and vertical seamlines to create a quilted grid (black lines).
Stitch additional straight lines at random parallel intervals in both directions to subdivide the space (red
lines). Continue quilting horizontal and vertical lines until you are pleased with the line spacing (blue lines).

BONUS IDEAS

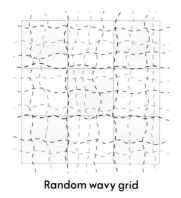

Random wavy grid

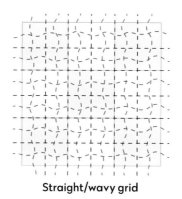

Straight/wavy grid

Wavy Crosshatch

See Diagonal Wavy Grid
(page 110).

Quilt wavy diagonals in both
directions across the quilt at
regular intervals.

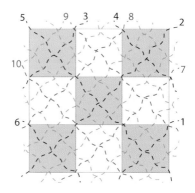

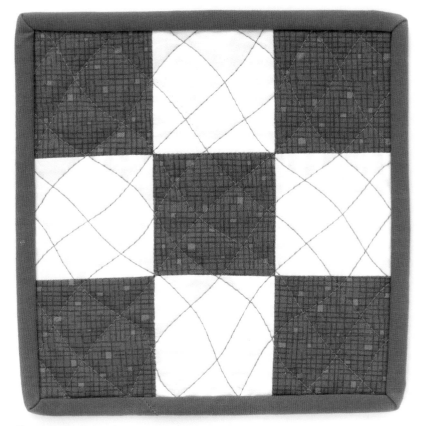

Photo by C&T Publishing, Inc.

Start with a wider interval between lines depending on the size of the block, and use the major block units as
guidelines for spacing (black lines). Quilt another pass of wavy lines subdividing the previous unquilted area
in half (red lines). Continue subdividing the area until you are pleased with the quilting density (blue lines).

BONUS IDEAS

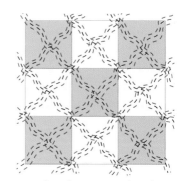

Echoed wavy crosshatch

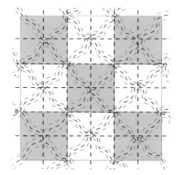

**Echoed wavy crosshatch
with straight line grid**

Echo Lines

See Angles & Curves (page 118).

Quilt the major seamlines of the area you wish to echo. Then quilt additional lines approximately ¼" to ½" away from the ditch or previously stitched line, depending on the width of your presser foot. This sample is a more extreme example of echoing with lots of turning and more stops and starts, but anything is possible when you choose to echo quilt!

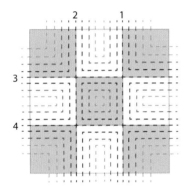

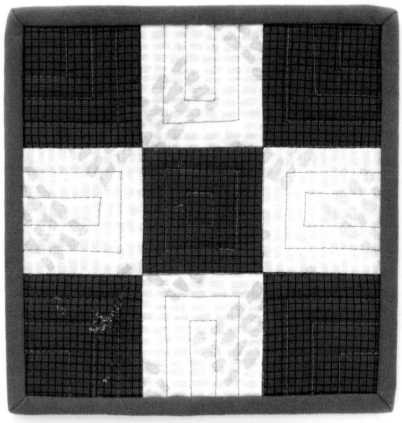

Photo by C&T Publishing, Inc.

After stitching in the ditch, quilt one set of echo lines next to each ditch you wish to draw attention to (black lines). Line up the edge of your presser foot against the previously quilted line and quilt another echo (red lines). Continue echo quilting until you've achieved your desired density (blue lines).

TIP / **To pivot at the corners, leave the needle in the down position, rotate, and check the position of the edge of your foot before beginning the next line of stitching. You might need to rotate back to your previous position, take one more stitch and then pivot again to make sure the edge of the foot lines up exactly with your previous line of stitching.**

BONUS IDEAS

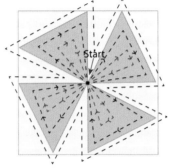

Echo any patchwork shape
(inside or outside or both).

Echo any walking-foot
quilting motif.

Free-Motion Quilting

Free-motion quilting requires different muscle movement than walking-foot quilting, but it's more flexible because you can stitch in any direction.

Free-motion work is like penmanship and everyone's quilting style varies. That's the beauty of "hand-crafted" machine quilting—no two motifs are exactly alike!

FREE-MOTION QUILTING PRACTICE

For this type of quilting, you need a specialty presser foot (see Presser Feet, page 14) and you must be able to drop, or disengage the feed dogs, which means they are not pulling the quilt through the machine. Therefore, if you put a quilt under the machine and don't move it around, you will simply stitch in place. The length of your stitches will depend on how fast you stitch relative to how fast or slow you push the quilt through the machine.

Some free-motion machines come with a stitch regulator which allows you to set a specified stitch length so you can experiment to see what you like. I personally don't worry too much about keeping my stitch length perfectly uniform as it's nearly impossible to do manually; therefore, I admire the beauty of imperfect quilting!

Getting Started

Scribble stitching • Photo by C&T Publishing, Inc.

Drop or cover your feed dogs and attach a free-motion foot that fits your machine (refer to your machine's instruction manual). On a practice sample, pull up the bobbin thread and start stitching in the batting to catch your threads, then move into the main stitching area of the sample. "Scribble" stitch your way around the area by moving the sample in any direction: up and down, left and right, back and forth, and on the diagonal. Do *not* try to form a specific design. Instead, get comfortable moving smoothly in all directions and work your way around the entire practice sample. You are trying to gently push the quilt or practice sample through the machine at a relatively even speed while staying in control.

When you feel like you are starting to reach the end, stop stitching with your needle in the down position on the practice sample. Reposition your hands comfortably around the needle, and continue your scribble practice. You might only stitch a few inches at a time before it's time to stop stitching and reposition your hands again. I like to think of my hands as a hoop and only concentrate on the small area in between.

TIP Where you place your hands on the quilt is a personal preference. Some quilters like to keep their hands flat on the surface of the quilt, using the palms of their hands to move the quilt. Others like to rest their fingertips on the quilt surface and apply downward pressure to move the quilt. Still others prefer to grasp a chunk of quilt in their hands while making a fist. There's no right or wrong hand position—only what feels most comfortable to you!

Hands flat, palms push or pull the quilt

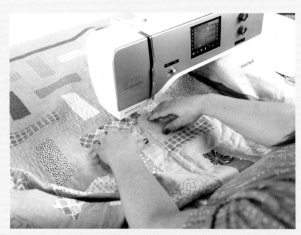

Fingertips push or pull the quilt as needed

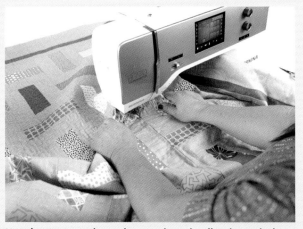

Hands grasping the quilt to push and pull it through the machine

Try It!

» To keep things flowing smoothly, scrunch up some of the surrounding quilt outside of your stitch area so that the area in between your hands is nice and flat. I call this "peaks and valleys." The valley is the area to be stitched, surrounded by mountain peaks of scrunched-up quilt.

Quilting gloves make it easier to form the peaks and valleys, and to push and pull the quilt through the machine.

» As you stitch, get comfortable with the way your needle moves, and how much pressure you need to put on the practice sample or quilt to move it around in a smooth, fluid motion. Be careful to keep your fingers out of the way while stitching!

» Try stitching faster or slower until you find a comfortable speed where you can stay in control. If your stitches look too small, push the sample through the machine a little bit faster to lengthen the stitches. If your stitches look too long, slow down your pushing movement so you can make more stitches in a smaller space. This will take a bit of practice to find the right rhythm, so don't give up if it feels awkward after the first few tries. "Scribble" the entire sample until you feel comfortable moving around in all directions. Try quilting straight-ish lines and also curvy lines as you practice staying in control.

» Sketching the design on paper first allows you to practice "muscle memory" to train your brain on how to move around a defined area. If you sketch out each and every design on paper before you quilt it free-form on a practice sample, your quilting practice will be more effective and you'll get noticeably better with each sample you stitch! Commit to sketching and stitching one sample a day for several days in a row, and you'll start to notice the improvement in no time!

» Practice free-motion quilting each design randomly on a practice sample, or combine designs as you feel comfortable. Some designs work better as an allover meander, winding your way around the area in a random way. Others work best when quilted between defined areas such as the seamlines of a block. Take note of other free-motion designs you've seen on other quilts or in photos—how would you translate those designs into a sketch and then into your own personal practice?

» When you are ready to practice quilting the free-motion designs (page 50), remember to sketch it, then stitch it. Fill up an entire sheet of paper with your drawn design and practice changing directions as you doodle, filling in all the spaces. Think about how you will get in and out of tight corners and in which direction you want to move next. Once you are comfortable with the flow of the design, try quilting something similar on a practice sample. Just remember; you aren't drawing on the quilt sample itself, and you aren't trying to replicate your drawn design exactly.

GALLERY OF FREE-MOTION QUILTING DESIGNS

Most of the free-motion designs on the following pages are used in one of the quilting plans in this book. As you practice sketching your designs on paper, and then translate those designs onto fabric, try various sizes of each motif, depending on the scale you want to quilt them.

Doodle Designs

See Doodle Flowers (page 82).

Quilt your favorite doodle meander like loops, then randomly add a whimsical design such as flowers or butterflies.

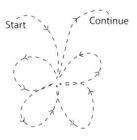

The secret to the success of this design is isolating the flower motif. Add a curved stem at the beginning and end of each set of flower petals. Begin on one side of the stem, draw or stitch 2 petals on the left, 2 petals on the right and then finish with another stem on the other side.

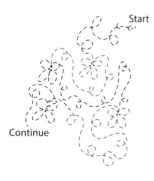

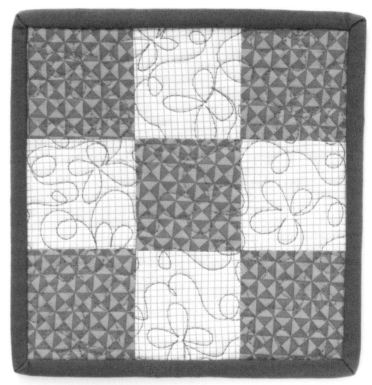

Photo by C&T Publishing, Inc.

Pick an area to start quilting and stitch a few random loops. Then quilt a flower with a stem in any direction. Quilt a few more loops—the number doesn't matter—and then another flower. Continue meandering the motif switching between loops and flowers as desired. Your design may look more like butterflies with just 4 petals. Try 5 or more petals for a different look.

BONUS IDEAS

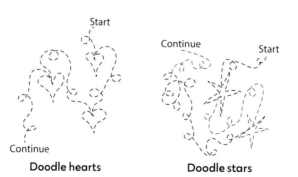

Doodle hearts   **Doodle stars**

Stipple Meander

See Chain Links (page 86).

Meander your way in and around the block in any direction until the area is completely quilted.

The design can be random, regardless of the seamlines. Or you can stitch into and out of one area at a time, moving from section to section at the points where the corners meet.

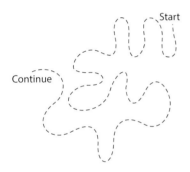

Quilt a meander design by stitching a series of bumpy or wavy lines that spread out in all directions. To get started, quilt 2–3 bumps in one area, then switch directions and continue in another area. If you get stuck, be sure to pause and think about where you want to move next.

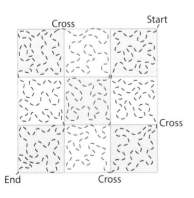

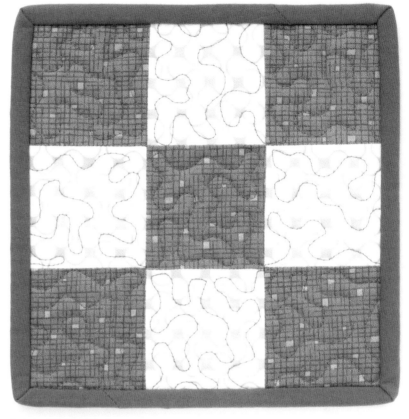

Photo by C&T Publishing, Inc.

To quilt precisely in one area of the block, fill in the immediate space with the meander design. Get to the next section of the block by stitching through the corner or point where two fabrics intersect. Continue quilting one section at a time before moving onto the next.

BONUS IDEAS

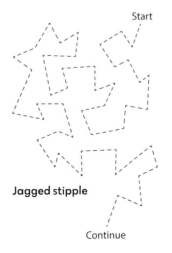

Jagged stipple

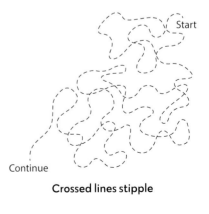

Crossed lines stipple

Continuous Curves

See Chain Links (page 86).

Bounce around the block quilting a smoothly curving line from corner to corner. The lines do not need to be perfectly smooth or equally spaced.

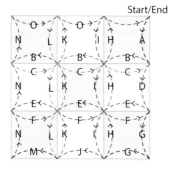

Plan out ahead of time how you will move around the block with the fewest starts and stops. For the 9-patch grid, stitch the curves in the order shown here, A–O. The letters indicate when the design changes directions.

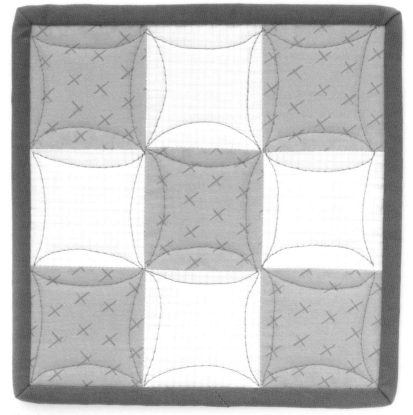

BONUS IDEAS

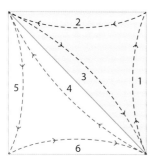

Continuous curves in triangles

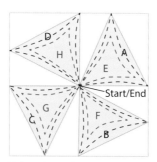

Echoed continuous curves

Circuits Meander

See Circuit Board (page 98).

This is another meander motif that can go in any direction to fill up the space. Think about where you want to start and stop the design to get to the next area to quilt. It's okay to overlap the design into other areas of the quilt as you stitch.

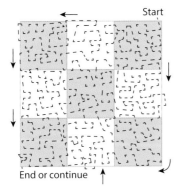

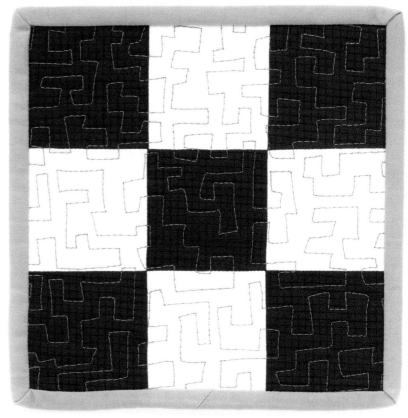

Photo by C&T Publishing, Inc.

Draw or stitch a series of rect-angular shapes that don't close completely. Try to stitch right angles when changing directions, but don't stress if you end up with points or other funky shapes. This design will be unique each time you stitch it! Quilt methodically down one area and up another to stay organized. It's okay to occasionally quilt off the side of the quilt or practice sample.

BONUS IDEAS

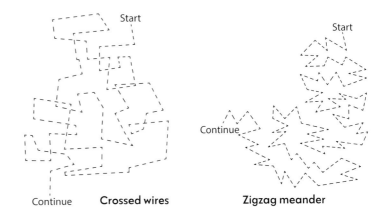

Crossed wires   **Zigzag meander**

Ruler Lines

See Fire & Ice (page 102).

When free-motion quilting straight lines, you can use a specialty acrylic ruler that's placed next to a specialty free-motion "ruler" foot to get precise line placement. The ruler and foot are thicker than the standard tools to ensure the foot won't slide under or on top of the ruler and damage your machine. Consult your manual to determine whether you need a "high-shank" or "low-shank" ruler and foot combination. These specialty tools can be found at most independent quilt shops. Working with a ruler can create precise straight lines without the need for a walking foot. Keep in mind that the stitched line will be approximately ¼″ away from the edge of the presser foot. Unlike a walking foot, these straight lines can be stitched in any direction without rotating the quilt.

Photo by C&T Publishing, Inc.

The "jewel box" ruler work design can be combined with other free-motion motifs to easily move in and around each area without the need to stop and cut thread. Use the same thread throughout. The trick is to back-track in the corners to continue the design.

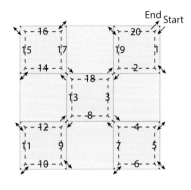

Meander quilt your way over to the starting point of the first jewel box motif. Quilt a short straight line at the corner to start. Quilt a straight line approximately ¼″ away from a side seam inside the block. Back-track in the corners before moving on to the next line to stitch. In this 9-patch example, follow the stitching path to quilt lines 1–20. Note the direction of the arrows to get in and out of each square.

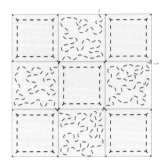

After stitching the jewel box motif in each section, fill in the other blank areas with a fun free-motion motif, such as stip-pling. Remember to get into and out of each area at the corners for a continuous stitching path. If desired, you can also fill in the jewel box squares with more echo lines, or another design.

BONUS IDEAS

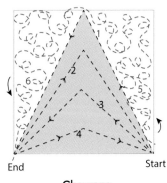

Chevrons
(with background fill)

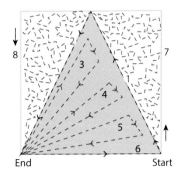

Point-to-point triangles
(with background fill)

Pointy Waves

See Fire & Ice (page 102).

Wavy lines can meander horizontally to form waves, vertically to form fire, or in any direction you choose. Get comfortable starting anywhere on the block for more flexibility in moving around your quilt. You can vary the number of lines quilted in each section for a more whimsical look!

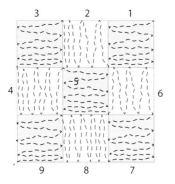

Draw or stitch a series of random wavy lines up and down or back and forth. When it's time to stitch in the opposition direction, form a sharp point at each end. Quilt an odd number of lines to keep moving in the direction in which you started. Quilt an even number of lines to change direction. With your finger, follow the stitching path shown to understand how the design flows continuously across the block.

Photo by C&T Publishing, Inc.

TIP If you will be stitching this design next to the edge of your quilt, you can account for the seam allowances and stop about ¼″ away from the edge. Or continue stitching to the edge and allow the points to get chopped off for a more organic look.

BONUS IDEAS

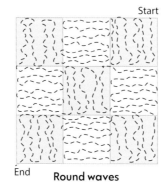

Round waves

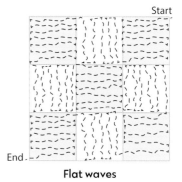

Flat waves

Wavy Chevrons

See Fire & Ice (page 102).

Wavy lines can be stitched in a variety of shapes to fill in areas of the quilt without measuring or marking. The trick to quilting them continuously is to quilt additional lines to fill in the gaps and move around the area you are quilting. Don't try to match the points of the chevrons; let them be free-form and random for a more modern look!

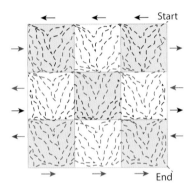

Quilt a chevron design by stitching an odd number of wavy lines to form the first chevron. Quilt one pass across the area you are filling in (see black lines, 1st row). Quilt back the other direction, filling in the gaps with more wavy lines and chevron shapes (red lines, 1st row). Switch directions again to quilt the next section (blue lines, 2nd row), and switch again to complete the next row (black lines, 2nd row). Finally, switch directions again to complete the last section (red lines, 3rd row and blue lines, 3rd row).

Photo by C&T Publishing, Inc.

TIP If at any time you get stuck and don't know where to stitch next, go ahead and stitch in the ditch to travel to the next section you need to quilt. You can also backtrack (stitch on top of a previous stitching line) if needed.

BONUS IDEAS

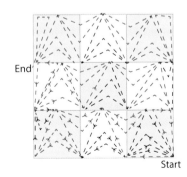

Straight-"ish" chevrons

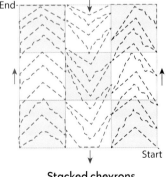

Stacked chevrons (straight and wavy)

Braided Chain

See Fire & Ice (page 102).

This is a great border or sashing design. It can be stretched or elongated, made narrower or wider as needed to fill the desired space.

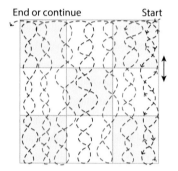

Quilt a wavy line in one direction with pronounced but random lumps and bumps. When you reach the end point, stitch back the other direction, crossing over the previous wavy line to form an irregular cable design.

TIP Remember you can really mix up these ideas. Stitch these designs horizontally, vertically, or even diagonally. Start on one side of the block/quilt or the other. End on the same side, or the opposite side, depending on where you need to travel on your quilt. Remember—the more irregular and whimsical they look, the easier they will be to stitch!

Photo by C&T Publishing, Inc.

BONUS IDEAS

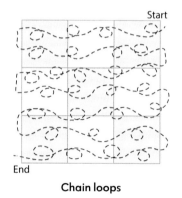

Chain loops

Double chain loops

Crackle Meander

See Crackle Pop! (page 114).

This meander design is very choppy, angular, and geometric. Slow down while drawing and while stitching to close up all the shapes.

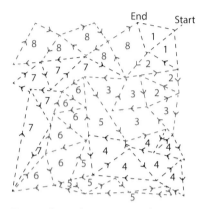

Remember—this is just an idea— yours may look completely different!

Begin with a straight choppy line. Make a closed triangle shape and veer off in another direction to form the next shape. Think about which direction you need to move to fill in the entire area. It's okay if you create lots of different geometric shapes as you form this design. Backtrack if necessary, to get out of a corner or to switch directions.

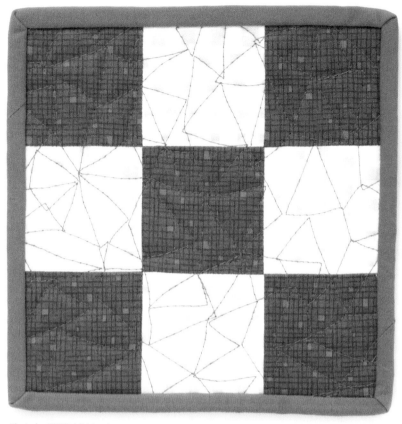

Photo by C&T Publishing, Inc.

BONUS IDEAS

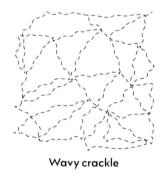

Wavy crackle

Shattered glass

Pebbles

See Chain Links (page 86) and Angles & Curves (page 118).

Pebbles are very dense so quilt them sparingly. Combine them with other shapes like snails (spirals), circles, and squares for a more playful look!

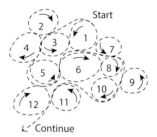

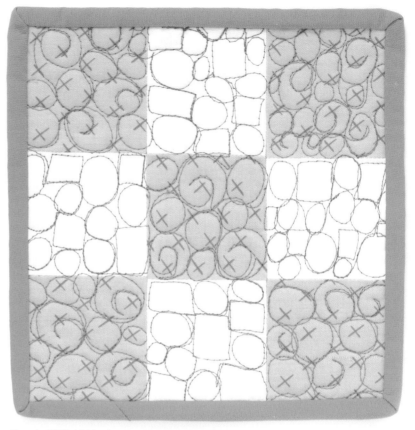

Photo by C&T Publishing, Inc.

Stitch a circle in one direction. Partially backtrack on the circle, switch directions, and quilt another circle right next to the previous one. Continue alternating directions and vary the size of the pebbles for interest. It's okay to leave gaps in the pebbles and stitch around a previous line as needed to change directions. They don't need to look perfect. Aim for texture over perfection here.

BONUS IDEAS

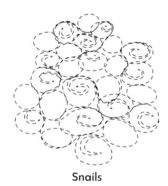

Snails

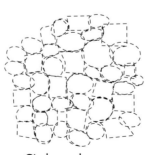

Circles and squares

Ribbon Candy

See Angles & Curves (page 118).

Ribbon Candy can be stitched from left to right, right to left, vertically, or horizontally. It can also bend around shapes as needed. If you start stitching the design in the wrong direction, or overlap the design, you may end up with Lazy 8's or Crazy 8's instead, and that's ok, too!

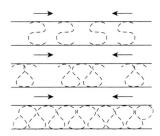

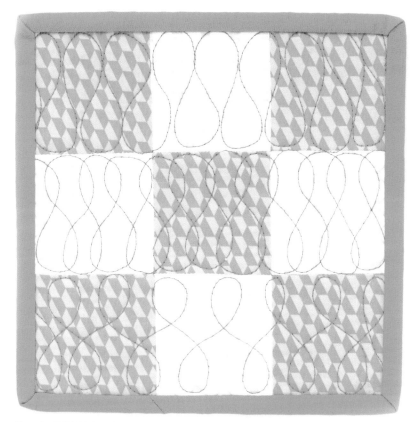

Photo by C&T Publishing, Inc.

Draw a series of "S" shapes and backward "S" shapes to form this design. They should nestle into each other. You can extend the curve at the start and stop of the design to make a clean finish (see red lines).

TIP To get comfortable with a more intricate design, trace over the design with your finger backwards and forwards. Rotate the page so that the design flows vertically and retrace with your finger to get a feel for the design flow at a different angle. Draw or stitch a small section of the design at a time, then pause and think about where you want to go next. Take your time with these designs and you'll be an expert in no time!

BONUS IDEAS

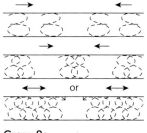

Crazy 8s

or

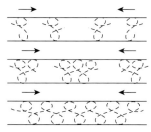

Lazy 8s

Switchbacks

See Angles & Curves (page 118).

This design is great for adding texture in smaller spaces. The lines looked best when they are quilted in areas that are 3″ tall or less. For larger areas, quilt additional rows of stacked switchbacks. They are also a fun design to weave in and out of a 9-patch or checkerboard pattern. The trick is figuring out where to stop, start, and rotate the design to fit your allotted space.

Photo by C&T Publishing, Inc.

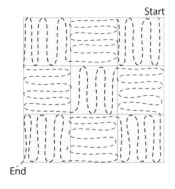

Draw or stitch a series of u and n shapes to form this design. Don't worry about quilting the same number of repeats in each section of your quilt. Start or end the design in the "up" or "down" position, depending on where you need to stitch next. Rotate or bend the design as needed to create a woven or stacked effect. Plan out your quilting so that you can fill in an entire area with only one start and stop.

BONUS IDEAS

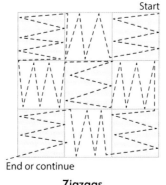

Zigzags

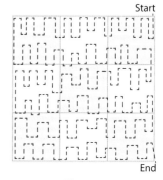

Zippers

Make a Quilting Plan

I love making a quilting plan for each and every quilt I create! It makes the whole process faster, easier, and "sew" much more fun!

A quilting plan is a rough sketch of the designs you plan to quilt on your quilt, along with the stitching pathway you'll take to move around the quilt. These sketches may be simple doodles on a piece of paper, or they may be more complex designs drawn onto a printed picture or photocopy of the pieced quilt design. Whether you will be free-motion quilting or quilting with a walking foot, a quilting plan is a good idea.

Depending on the complexity of the quilt, you may choose to enlarge an image of the pieced blocks to plan out the quilting in detail. Each of the 3 projects in this book (page 71) include 3 different quilting plans: allover walking foot, allover free-motion, and custom quilting. These will help build your skills as you become a better machine quilter.

WHY MAKE A QUILTING PLAN?

Planning the quilting ahead of time allows you to enjoy the actual machine stitching process, without worrying about whether your ideas will work or not. I find that once I get all the thinking out of the way by formulating a plan, I can sit back, relax, and enjoy the "zen" feeling I get when I'm in the zone of mindless machine quilting. It's an enjoyable rhythm that's easily achieved when I'm not constantly fretting about what to do next.

However, don't be so rigid in your plans that you can't deviate from your original idea. Even though you make a quilting plan and/or a practice sample ahead of time, on occasion you may find that you want to go in a different direction than originally intended. If you are ever stumped on coming up with a design for your quilting plan, only plan part of the design, stitch it out, and then plan more after that particular section is done.

A quilting plan is just another tool in your arsenal to make machine quilting more fun, enjoyable, and stress-free!

Divide and Conquer

The best way to plan your quilting is to divide up the stitching design into manageable steps and conquer one section of quilting at a time. You'll "anchor" or secure the quilt in a few key places, allowing you to go back and add as much quilting as you'd like in any area of the quilt later. It's easiest to start on the right-hand side of the quilt and work your way towards the middle of the quilt. When you reach the center, rotate the quilt 180° and continue quilting from the center, back to the right-hand side. It's much easier to handle the bulk this way because you are easing into it a few inches at a time. See A Simple Quilting Plan below for an explanation of the Divide and Conquer process.

A Simple Quilting Plan

This easy quilting plan of edge-to-edge wavy lines is a bonus design for you to get comfortable with the process. Photocopy the Daisy Chain quilt (page 76) so that you can sketch out this plan on paper first. If desired, follow a similar pathway when it's time to quilt the real quilt! Remember, you aren't marking the stitch lines on your quilt; the number of lines you quilt will most likely be different from the number indicated on your plan.

1. Begin with a wavy line on the major vertical seam that's furthest to the right on your quilt. For example, Daisy Chain measures 90″ × 90″ and each full row of blocks measures 10″. So, the first line you'll quilt is approximately 10″ away from the right edge of the quilt, accounting for the border and partial blocks. The next line you'll quilt is 20″ away from the right edge, then 30″ away, and so on. Keep going until you've quilted these "anchor" lines halfway across the quilt. See black lines 1–4.

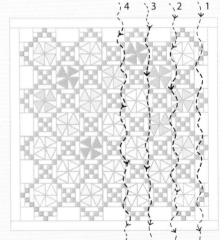

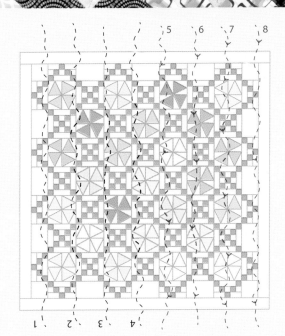

2. Next, rotate the quilt so that the previously quilted lines (1–4) are to your left. Notice that the numbers are now at the bottom of the plan, indicating that what used to be the top of the quilt is now at the bottom, from your perspective. The unquilted area is to your right. Begin quilting the next line at the center top of the quilt, where you left off previously. This will evenly distribute the quilting across the quilt. Work your way from the center of the quilt to the right, quilting each major seamline between the rows. Stitch randomly on top of or near the ditch for a more organic look. See red lines 5–8.

3. You've just completed the first pass across the quilt. For the next pass across the quilt, roughly divide each space in half so that the wavy lines are now approximately 5″ apart. Stitch the next set of lines in between each of the previous lines 1–8. (See blue lines drawn in between each of the red lines).

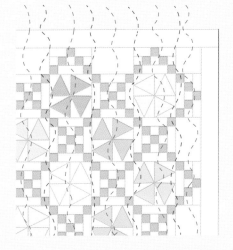

4. Continue by subdividing the space again and again until you are happy with the line spacing. Depending on the design of your quilt, you may choose to divide the quilting lines based on the actual seams of your quilt rather than exactly in half with each pass across the quilt. For example, the triangle units in Daisy Chain are 5″ apart while each of the square chain units are 2″ apart. And the borders are only 4″ wide.

Therefore, you can draw or stitch your wavy lines this way:

- 10″ apart between blocks/rows
- 5″ apart through the middle of the triangle pinwheel blocks and 9 patch blocks
- 4″ away from the edge for the border seams
- 2″ apart between the smaller squares

In some areas, the lines won't be equally spaced, but that's okay. Your eye will focus on the overall texture rather than measuring how accurately each line has been stitched.

Study the nine quilting plans, shown on the three quilt projects that follow to see how this basic technique is modified to fit each design. Then think about how you can apply similar techniques to any quilt in your UFO (Unfinished Fabric Object) pile!

The three quilt projects include Daisy Chain (page 72), Loose Weave (page 90), and Pinwheel Tessellation (page 106).

CONTROLLING THE BULK

Contrary to popular belief, you can start quilting anywhere on the quilt if your quilt is well basted. I prefer to start on the right-hand side of the quilt and work my way to the center, then rotate the quilt and finish quilting the other half of the quilt.

It is easiest to control the bulk of the quilt by starting your quilting on one edge and moving methodically across the quilt. You'll never need to scrunch more than half the quilt under the machine at any one time and this process allows you to slowly build up the bulk under the machine as you go. As you quilt, you'll start with most of the bulk of the quilt to your left, and a small amount of the quilt under the needle. At this point, none of the quilt is accumulating in the harp space to your right, so you won't feel confined.

The quilt bulk to your left should be resting on your sewing table and any other large surface you've placed around you to hold the weight of the quilt. Some of the quilt may be in your lap waiting to be pushed through the machine. As you begin stitching your design, work methodically from the top of the quilt (upper right), to the bottom of the quilt, depending on your quilting plan. As you stitch your way across each row or area of the quilt, you'll add more bulk to your right (under the arm of the machine), and reduce the bulk to your left.

It's easiest to start quilting on the right edge of your quilt.

1. For example, if you are quilting an 80″ wide quilt, you might start by quilting up to 10″ of the quilt on the right-hand side. This means that there's 10″ of quilt scrunched under the machine and 70″ of quilt spread out on the table to your left. Easy peasy, right? That's not too much bulk to deal with and you are gaining confidence as you stitch. As you methodically quilt your design, the bulk to your right will get bigger, and the bulk to your left will get smaller, until you have about half of the quilt (40″) squeezed and shoved into the harp space of your machine. The wonderful thing about this method is that you are slowly increasing the bulk under the machine a few inches at a time, rather than shoving half of the quilt through your machine all at once in the beginning.

As you stitch, scrunch the quilted section under the arm of the machine to your right.

2. Now the bulk of the quilt to your right has been stitched, and the remaining bulk of the quilt to your left has not yet been quilted. When you've quilted about half of the quilt, rotate it 180° and scrunch up the unquilted half under the machine and to your right. The quilted half will now be off to your left and you can unfurl it and let it relax, or move it out of the way.

Smoosh and rotate once you've stitched about half of the quilt.

3. Continue quilting multiple passes across the quilt according to your quilting plan until the quilting design is complete. Depending on the plan you choose, your anchor quilting lines may be more widely spaced, or closer together. When doing an allover free-motion quilting plan, there are no anchor lines at all because you quilt the entire design as you go, block by block, securing each part of the quilt as you get to it.

Continue stitching the unquilted half of the quilt that's now under the arm of the machine.

The important thing to remember is to focus on the small area of quilt that you are stitching. You are likely to spend more time scrunching, smooshing and rearranging the quilt rather than stitching, and that's perfectly okay. Enjoy the process and take pride in the fact that you are doing it yourself!

Photos by C&T Publishing, Inc.

PROJECTS TO *Practice* YOUR SKILLS

The following pages feature complete step-by-step instructions on how to piece the quilt top for three different projects: Daisy Chain, Loose Weave, and Pinwheel Tessellation, each with 3 different options on how to quilt them. Choose allover walking-foot quilting, edge to edge free-motion quilting, or custom quilting which combines both walking-foot quilting and free-motion techniques.

The patterns are loosely based on pinwheel blocks, which present a lot of movement. However, you can easily adapt any of the following quilting plans to other quilts you are working on. Moreover, you can substitute any of the walking-foot or free-motion motifs for even more possibilities. By breaking down the process, you'll finish more quilts, and have fun doing it!

Daisy Chain

FINISHED BLOCK: 10″× 10″ · FINISHED QUILT: 90″× 90″

Daisy Chain combines 2 interesting blocks based on different pieced grids. This means fewer seams to match up, and lots of blocks to show off your favorite prints. All 3 versions of this quilt are sewn from similar fabrics to demonstrate how machine quilting impacts the pieced design.

MATERIALS LIST

Fabric is based on 40″ of usable width.
One fat eighth = 9″ × 20″.

- 6½ yards of gray/white back-ground fabric

- 2¼ yards of dark blue for chains and binding

- 25 fat eighths of assorted colorful prints for daisy blocks, or scraps to total that amount

- 9 yards of fabric for backing (less if you decide to use leftovers on the back)

- 98″ × 98″ piece of batting

- Approximately 2400 yards of thread for machine quilting

- *Recommended:* Specialty rulers for making triangle-in-a-square blocks, or template making material (I use the Tri-Recs tool.)

CUTTING

TIP **Use leftover fabric for the back by sewing scraps into larger pieced chunks. Or throw them into your scrap stash to use for another project.**

Cutting the Daisy Blocks

Follow the instructions in Triangle Cutting (page 74).

From each fat eighth

- Cut 1 strip 5½″ × 20″.

- Subcut each strip into 4 center triangles that are 5½″ tall. Repeat to cut a total of 100 center triangles (4 per fat eighth).

From the background fabric

- Cut 10 strips 5½″ × 40″.

- Cut 100 triangle pairs (100 left and 100 right). *See "Triangle Cutting" on next page.*

Cutting the Chains, Background, and Binding

From the background fabric

- Cut 7 strips 6½″ × 40″.

  Subcut 12 rectangles 6½″ × 10½″ and 4 squares 6½″ × 6½″.

  Subcut 48 rectangles 2½″ × 6½″.

- Cut 10 strips 4½″ × 40″ for the border.

- Cut 4 strips 6½″ × 40″ for strip piecing.

- Cut 2 strips 4½″ × 40″ for strip piecing.

- Cut 12 strips 2½″ × 40″ for strip piecing.

TIP **For the most efficient use of your fabric, cut the larger back-ground rectangles first, and then the smaller ones from the remain-ing partial strips.**

From the dark blue fabric

- Cut 20 strips 2½″ × 40″ for the blocks.

- Cut 10 strips 2″ × 40″ for the binding (or wider as desired).

Daisy Chain

Triangle Cutting

See triangle templates (page 126). Layer up to 4 strips at a time to cut faster.

Cutting Center Triangles

For faster cutting, layer up to 4 strips.

1. Align the 5½″ line of the ruler or template with the bottom edge of a 5½″ × 20″ fabric strip. The top blunted point of the ruler should be aligned with the top of the strip. Make sure there is fabric extending beyond both sides of the triangle.

2. Rotary cut along the left edge of the ruler to cut the first triangle edge.

3. Rotary cut along the right edge of the ruler to release the triangle.

Cutting Side Triangle Pairs

You should be able to cut 10 pairs of triangles per strip.

1. Once the 5½″ × 40″ strips are cut, keep them folded (5½″ × 20″) so they are two layers thick. This ensures that you cut a complete pair—one left triangle and one right triangle—with each cut.

2. Align the 5½″ line of the ruler or template with the bottom edge of the 5½″ wide fabric strip. The top of the ruler should be aligned with the top edge of the strip.

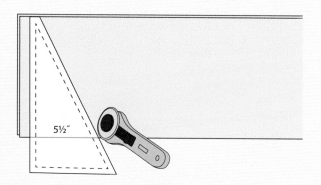

4. Rotate the ruler or template 180° so the 5½″ line is now aligned with the top edge of the fabric strip, and the blunted point of the ruler is aligned with the bottom of the strip. The diagonal edge should be aligned with the last cut.

5. Rotary cut along the right edge of the ruler. Repeat to cut as many center triangles as needed.

3. Cut along both sides of the triangle.

4. Rotate the ruler or template 180° so the diagonal edge lines up with the last cut and the blunted tip is aligned with the bottom edge of the strip.

5. Cut along the straight edge. Repeat to cut as many triangle pairs as needed.

MAKE THE QUILT TOP

Seam allowances are ¼″ and all seams are pressed open.

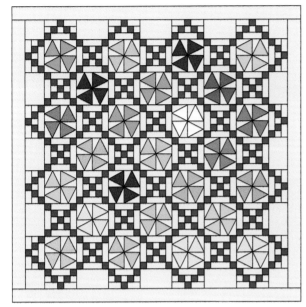

Quilt top assembly

TIP / When piecing my quilts, I prefer to press all the seams open to create square, flat blocks with seams that are much easier to match and join. This eliminates much of the bulk which makes it much easier to machine quilt with no lumps and bumps. Sew with a shorter stitch length (2.0 instead of 2.5) to prevent the seams from splitting, and pin generously at the intersections to match the seams.

Make the Daisy Blocks

1. Sew one left and one right background triangle to either side of one center triangle.

Correct orientation

Wrong!

If you trim off the side triangle tips, they will align properly in the corners.

TIP / Double-check that the triangles are oriented correctly. The blunt end of each triangle pair should be at the bottom. The blunt end of the center triangle should be at the top.

2. Repeat to make 4 triangle-in-a-square units from each fabric, for a total of 100 units. The units should measure 5½″ square unfinished.

3. Join 4 triangle-in-a-square units following the orientation shown to make one Daisy block that spins right (R). Repeat to make a total of 13 R's that measure 10½″ square unfinished.

4. Join 4 triangle-in-a-square units following the orientation below to make one Daisy block that spins left (L). Repeat to make a total of 12 L's that measure 10½″ square unfinished.

Make the Chain Blocks

Make a total of 24 complete Chain blocks and 16 partial Chain blocks.

TIP / **Always sew with the darker fabric on top. This reverses the sewing direction of each added strip to prevent the strip sets from warping or bowing out of shape.**

CREATE THE STRIP SETS

1. Sew 2 dark blue strips, 2½″ × 40″ to either side of 1 light background strip, 6½″ × 40″ to create strip set A. Repeat to make 4 of strip set A. Subcut into 64 pieced units, 2½″ × 10½″.

2. Sew 2 dark blue strips, 2½″ × 40″ to either side of 1 light background strip, 2½″ × 40″ to create strip set B. Repeat to make 3 of strip set B. Subcut into 48 pieced units, 2½″ × 6½″.

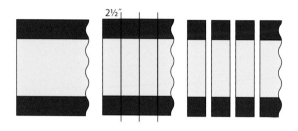

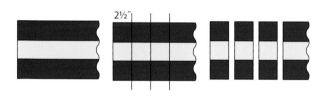

3. Sew 2 light background strips, 2½″ × 40″ to either side of 1 dark blue strip, 2½″ × 40″ to create strip set C. Repeat to make 3 of strip set C. Subcut into 40 pieced units, 2½″ × 6½″.

4. Sew 3 light background strips, 2½″ × 40″ and 2 dark blue strips, 2½″ × 40″, alternating colors to create 1 strip set D. Subcut into 16 pieced units, 2½″ × 10½″.

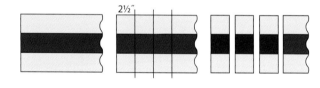

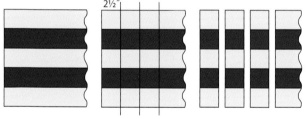

5. Sew a light background strip, 4½″ × 40″ on each side of 1 dark blue strip 2½″ × 40″ to create 1 strip set E. Subcut into 16 pieced units, 2½″ × 10½″.

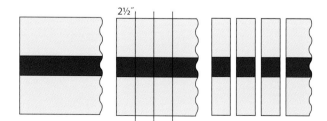

MAKE THE FULL CHAIN BLOCKS

1. Lay out 2 A units, 2 background rectangles 2½″ × 6½″, 2 B units, and 1 C unit as shown.

2. Sew the center block section together first by assembling the nine-patch unit and adding the 2 side background rectangles.

3. Join the top, middle, and bottom rows to complete a Chain block. Repeat to make a total of 24 full Chain blocks.

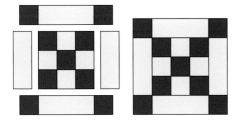

MAKE THE HALF CHAIN BLOCKS

1. Lay out 1 A unit, 1 D unit, and 1 E unit as shown.

2. Sew the units together to create a partial Chain block. Repeat to make a total of 16 partial Chain blocks.

Assemble the Quilt Top

1. Lay out all 25 Daisy blocks, 24 full chain blocks, 16 partial chain blocks, 12 background rectangles, and 4 corner background squares as shown.

2. Arrange into 9 rows of 9 blocks in a pleasing order. Be sure to alternate the Daisy blocks between L and R in each row.

TIP **Lay out your blocks on a design wall or other large surface. Take a picture with your phone to refer to as you sew.**

3. Sew blocks 2 at a time and join pairs of blocks into larger units until each row is complete.

4. Join the rows to complete the quilt top.

ASSEMBLE THE QUILT LAYERS AND QUILT 3 DIFFERENT WAYS

Refer to Preparing the Quilt (page 22) for how to assemble and baste the quilt layers and to Make a Quilt Plan.

Machine quilt Daisy Chain using one of these 3 quilting plans: Floral Spray, Doodle Flowers, or Chain Links. Feel free to mix and match them on a variety of other quilt patterns, too!

Walking-Foot Quilting Plan: Floral Spray

This quilting plan plays up the floral theme. The quilting lines radiating from the corner represent an abstract floral arrangement emanating from a vase, with the flowers spreading out to fill in all the spaces. When you draw your plan, you can mark each line you plan to quilt, or go for a more organic look with unmarked, free-form lines.

This plan is fast to stitch, fun to quilt, and adds a modern aesthetic to an otherwise traditional quilt pattern.

For best results, follow the quilting plan number order as indicated, but don't worry about stitching the exact number of lines indicated on the plan. Use it as more of a reference or general guideline to understand the overall design. If you look closely, you'll see that I've quilted my finished quilt with *many* more lines than shown on the original plan.

TIP If you choose to mark your lines, use a straight edge and water soluble marking pen. Or place several pieces of painter's tape across the quilt to act as stitching guides.

This quilting plan is rotated 180° so begin stitching in the upper right corner of the quilt.

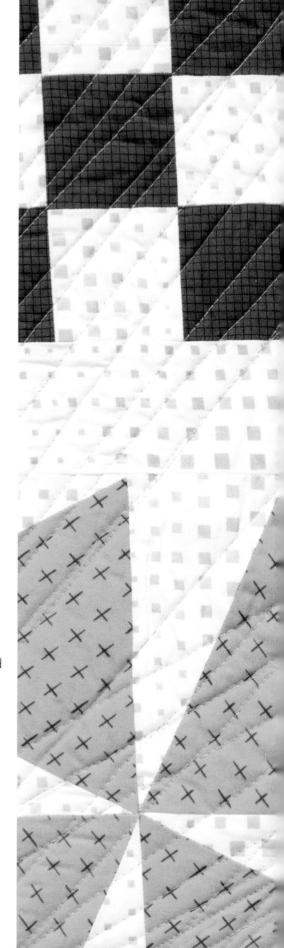

FIRST PASS ACROSS THE QUILT

Rotate the quilt to begin stitching at the top right corner of the quilt. Quilt a straight line across to the other edge of the quilt on the lower right. Rotate the quilt as needed so that you can stitch a few anchor lines diagonally across the quilt. See black lines 1–7, below.

Begin and end each line of stitching off the quilt, in the batting. There is no need to secure the starting and ending thread tails because they are trimmed away before the binding is applied.

The point of stitching a few lines first is to secure the quilt layers from shifting, and to ensure that the quilting texture is evenly distributed throughout the bulk of the quilt. You can always add more lines to your quilt to even out the spacing, but just remember that it's difficult to "unquilt" if you start off too densely in one area.

SECOND PASS ACROSS THE QUILT

Mark and then quilt another series of lines across the quilt to further divide the space.

You can evenly divide up the space in between each set of lines; or let the spacing be more organic and irregular.

TIP / **Mark each set of lines on the quilt right before you quilt them, just in case you decide to change your mind on how many to quilt.**

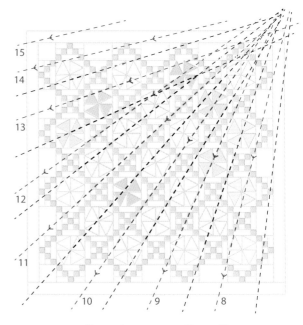

Second pass across the quilt

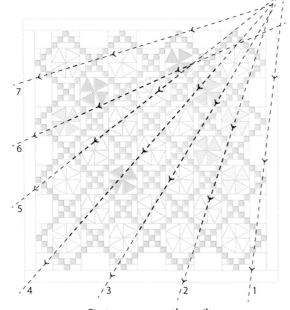

First pass across the quilt

ADDITIONAL PASSES ACROSS THE QUILT

Continue stitching more lines of quilting as desired. See blue lines on the quilting plan below.

Each time you quilt another set of lines across the quilt you can stop and determine if you'd like to keep going. It's completely up to you to decide when the quilt is "finished!"

TIP Be sure to keep an eye on your bobbin! The number of lines you can quilt on one bobbin may vary, but if you have a low bobbin indicator light, be sure to change it when the bobbin runs low, hopefully after you complete the current line of stitching you are working on.

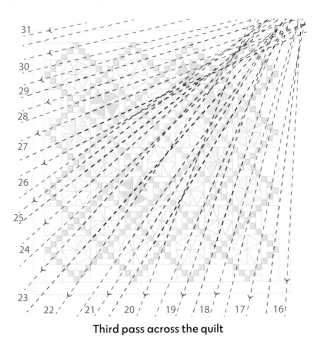

Third pass across the quilt

Note You can display this finished quilt with the lines going from upper right to bottom left, or you can rotate the quilt 180° so that the straight lines look like they are radiating from the bottom lower left corner of the quilt.

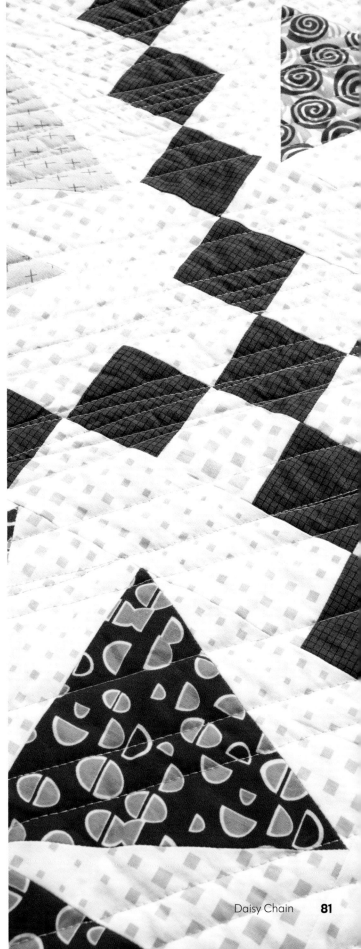

Free-Motion Quilting Plan: Doodle Flowers

This quilting plan plays up the floral theme but in a more traditional, cutesy way. Because this is a large quilt, the allover design finishes in a hurry while masking any piecing imperfections. If there are any trouble spots on your quilt where the seams don't line up, simply throw in a few extra doodles in that area!

Loops are one of the easiest designs to free-motion quilt and you can personalize them by throwing in a random motif that matches the theme of your quilt. Remember to draw out your quilting design on paper first so you can work out how to form the loops and add the bonus flower motif. See page 50.

Decide how large or small you want to quilt the Doodle Flowers and practice on a sample. I usually draw my motifs at a bigger scale on the quilting plan, then quilt them on a smaller scale on the real quilt to add lots of dense texture. Try to keep the density consistent across the quilt, no matter how large or small of a design you stitch.

ALLOVER MEANDERING

Start the design in the upper right-hand corner of the quilt and work your way down each row. When you get to the end of the first row, work your way back up the next row, and so on.

When quilting edge to edge free-motion designs, you'll quilt the design block by block in a methodical manner. Only focus on the block in front of you rather than the entire quilt so you don't get overwhelmed. Stitch the meandering loops and flowers up and down, side to side, and in all directions to cover the entire block area including the chain units and the triangle blocks. Treat the border as part of the overall design. Stitch each part of it with the same quilting motif as you make your way across the quilt.

To help the design blend in with the rest of the quilt, stitch some of it to your left, dipping into the next row of blocks, and possibly in the next block above or below. You want the texture to appear seamless, with no gaps in the quilting and without it looking like you created an obvious stitching path.

Continue stitching to the next adjacent block or area. When you have finished quilting the first couple of blocks including some of the surrounding area, be sure to stop with the needle in the down position in your quilt. Move the quilt and adjust your hand position so that you can select the next area to be stitched. You may need to adjust the quilt and your hands several times while quilting the same block area, depending on your reach. Always stop with the needle in the down position and anticipate where your needle will move so you can transition smoothly between starts and stops.

TIP Remember to check your bobbin often and get a feel for how many blocks you can quilt on one bobbin's worth of thread. Knowing this allows you to plan your exit strategy when it's time to change your bobbin. When your bobbin is running low, meander your way to the closest quilt edge and stitch off the side of the quilt, into the batting. Put in a fresh bobbin and meander your way back to the area you were filling in. The stitching path won't be noticeable, and you'll save the frustration of having to restart quilting in the middle of the quilt.

After a few bobbins' worth of thread, there may be lint buildup, which can prevent proper stitch formation, so be sure to clean and de-lint your machine regularly.

Continue quilting the Doodle Flowers design from block to block until the entire quilt is stitched. You can time yourself as you quilt one block; or make an extra block to use as a practice sample and take note of how long it takes to stitch. Then you can estimate how long it will take to quilt the entire thing. Remember to work from the right side of the quilt, scrunching up the quilted area to your right, under the machine.

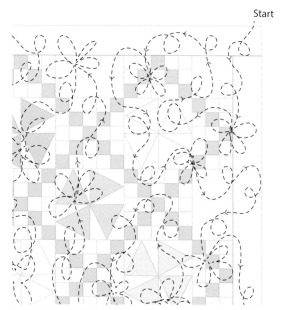

Start

Detail of Doodle Flowers quilting plan, not to scale

Rotate the quilt 180° after you've quilted about half of it, so that the bulk of the quilted area is now to your left as you continue working your way continuously across the quilt.

TIP/ If the task seems overwhelming, set a goal for yourself, perhaps covering one or two blocks per quilting session. This same technique of edge-to-edge quilting can be applied to any meandering free-motion design.

Custom Quilting Plan: Chain Links

Photos by C&T Publishing, Inc.

This plan creates that "wow" factor with custom quilting that is easier to stitch than it looks. Straight lines combined with curves create balance when quilting a symmetrical pieced design.

Chain Links combines the following:

» Straight Parallel Lines (page 43), which emphasize the diagonal grid created by the pieced chains.

» Stippling (page 51) in the background to add texture.

» Continuous Curves (page 52) for more interest in the triangle blocks.

Whenever I combine walking-foot quilting with free-motion quilting in the same quilt, I do all the walking-foot quilting first. This anchors and stabilizes the quilt, and then it's much easier to add free-motion designs later. I try to quilt the longest continuous line possible to reduce the number of starts and stops. Follow the step-by-step instructions to divide the design into multiple stitching paths, so you can easily conquer each task!

1. Quilt the straight-line diagonal grid with a walking foot to anchor your quilt.

Rotate the quilt 45° so that you can quilt diagonal lines through each of the chains. Quilt 3 (or more) sets of parallel lines through each diagonal chain, starting and ending off the quilt with each stitched line. Follow the path to quilt chains 1–4, then rotate the quilt 180 degrees. Next, quilt chains 5–8 going in the other direction. (From your perspective you will be quilting each line from the top of the quilt to the bottom.)

TIP The anchor lines don't need to be marked. You can simply eyeball them by stitching from point to point on the outer corner of each square. Or for faster, less fussy quilting, you can replace some or all the straight lines with wavy lines instead.

Quilt each diagonal line all the way across the quilt, including the border areas.

Rotate the quilt 90° clockwise and continue quilting parallel lines in chains 9–12. Rotate again to finish quilting parallel lines in chains 13–16. This completes the diagonal grid.

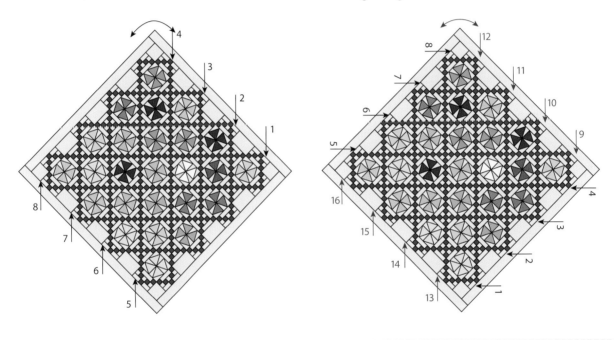

2. If desired, stitch in the ditch around each of the long blue chains. Start on one side of a chain and stitch a continuous path around the blue squares, rotating the quilt as needed until you complete the longest section you can. It's ok to backtrack in the seams to get to the next chain. Stitch all of the chains the same way.

3. Free-motion quilt the background and stitch continuous curves in the triangles.

Begin by stippling the background area in the upper corner of the quilt. Fill in the nearby border areas and the half-block backgrounds. Then free-motion stitch in the ditch through one of the seamlines to get to the first pinwheel block. Stipple in the background around the pinwheel and stitch to the center of the pinwheel where the triangle tips meet.

Quilt continuous curves by bouncing around each corner of the triangle and back to the starting point. Repeat to quilt all triangles this way. If desired, quilt another round of continuous curves inside each triangle, echoing the first set of lines. Exit the triangle unit in a different section of background and stipple quilt to fill in all remaining background space around the triangles. Follow the Pinwheel block quilting plan.

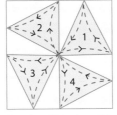

Pinwheel block quilting plan

If desired, quilt pebbles in the small background triangles between the blue squares. Follow the same general pathway you took to quilt the chains.

To divide and conquer, stitch each of the designs in this order—Walking foot: straight lines in the chains, optional stitch-in the ditch; Free-motion: stipple and curves in the pinwheels/backgrounds, optional pebbles. Backtrack in the seams between the blocks to get to the next area to quilt without cutting thread. Remember to rotate the quilt halfway through with each pass of the design so it's not too bulky under the machine.

TIP When quilting your way around each block, leave enough room so that you can get into and out of each area without crossing over an obvious quilting motif.

Loose Weave

FINISHED BLOCK: 6″× 6″ · FINISHED QUILT: 59″× 71″

Loose Weave is so fast to piece that it gives you more time to explore machine quilting ideas. Fabric selection is easy—just pick your favorite color story and pair it with a high contrasting background. But be warned, you'll probably want to make more than one!

MATERIALS LIST

Fabric is based on 40″ of usable width.

One precut strip = 2½″ × 40″.

3¼ yards of gray background fabric

¾ yards of coordinating color for accent border and binding

14 precut strips of coordinating colors for blocks, or scraps to total that amount (approximately 1 yd)

4 yards of fabric for backing

67″ × 79″ piece of batting

Approximately 1200 yards of thread for machine quilting

CUTTING

From gray background

• Cut 28 strips 2½″ × 40″ for the strip pieced blocks.

• Cut 6 strips 1½″ × 40″ for the inner border.

• Cut 7 strips 4″ × 40″ for the outer border.

From accent color

• Cut 6 strips 1½″ × 40″ for the accent border.

• Cut 7 strips 2″ × 40″ for the binding (or wider as desired).

MAKE THE QUILT TOP

Seam allowances are ¼″ and all seams are pressed open.

Make the Blocks

1. Sew 2 strips of gray background to either side of 1 colorful strip and press. Repeat to create 14 strip sets.

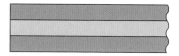

TIP Always sew with the colorful fabric strip on top. This reverses the sewing direction of each strip, which prevents the strip sets from warping or bowing out of shape.

2. Subcut each strip set into 6 units, 6½″ × 6½″ for a total of 80. (You'll have 4 left over you can save for another project.)

TIP For speedy sewing, sew together 2 blocks into a pair as shown below. Repeat to sew a total of 40 random pairs just like this. This will make it easier to lay out the blocks for quilt top assembly, while preserving the scrappy look. Rotate the block pairs as needed for quilt top assembly on page 93.

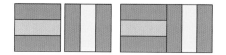

Quilt top assembly

Assemble the Quilt Top

1. Use a design wall or other large surface to lay out all blocks into a pleasing arrangement of 10 rows with 8 blocks each.

2. Sew the blocks together in each row and press.

3. Join the rows to complete the inner quilt top before the borders.

4. Join the 1½″ × 40″ gray inner border strips edge to edge, or on the diagonal to create one larger strip.

5. Measure each side of the quilt top and trim 2 gray strips to match this length. Mathematically they should measure 60½″. Sew inner gray borders to either side of the quilt top and press.

6. Measure the top and bottom of the quilt top and trim two gray strips to match this length. Mathematically they should measure 50½". Sew inner gray borders to the top and bottom and press.

7. Repeat Steps 4–6 with the accent color. Mathematically the side accent borders should measure 1½" × 62½". The top and bottom accent borders should measure 1½" × 52½".

8. Join the 4" × 40" strips together for outer borders.

9. Measure the 2 sides of the quilt and trim 2 strips to match. Mathematically this should be 64½". Sew borders to either side of the quilt and press.

10. Measure the top and bottom of the quilt and trim 2 strips to match. Mathematically this should be 59½". Sew borders to top and bottom and press to complete the quilt top.

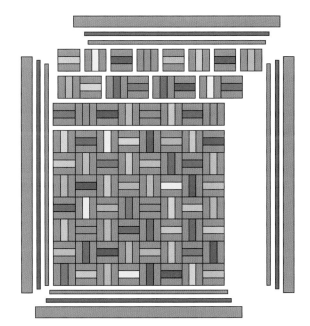

TIP / When piecing my quilts, I prefer to press all seams open to create square, flat blocks. This eliminates much of the bulk, which makes it easier to match the seams and enables you to machine quilt with no lumps and bumps. Sew with a shorter stitch length (2.0 instead of 2.5) to prevent the seams from splitting, and pin generously next to either side of the intersections to match the seams.

ASSEMBLE THE QUILT LAYERS AND QUILT 3 DIFFERENT WAYS

Refer to Preparing the Quilt (pages 22) for how to assemble and baste the quilt layers.

Machine quilt Loose Weave using one of these 3 quilting plans: Random Crosshatch, Circuit Board, or Fire & Ice. Feel free to mix and match them on a variety of other quilt patterns, too.

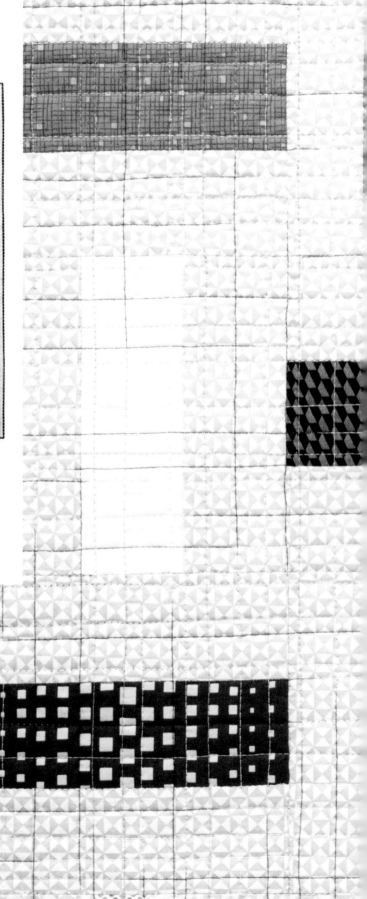

Walking-Foot Quilting Plan: Random Crosshatch

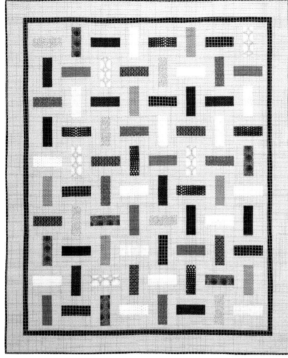

This quilting plan works well on any quilt that has a regular layout of blocks set into rows. The strong geometric quilting design unifies the black/white/gray contrast of this colorway in an edgy modern way.

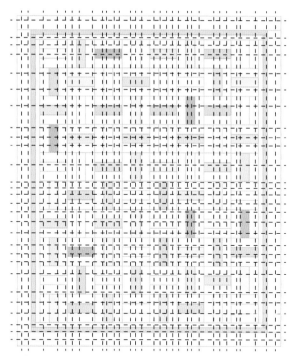

Refer to the quilting plan.

1. Anchor quilt between the block rows.

Starting on the right side of the quilt at the top, stitch a straight line in the border seam between the skinny inner border and the thicker outer border. Draw or crease a line from the top of the quilt to the point where the pieced border begins if needed.

Scrunch up the quilt and stitch another line in the ditch (page 42) between the inner border and the first vertical row of blocks. Quilt additional anchor lines in the ditch vertically between each block (about 6″ apart which is the finished block size). Quilt halfway across the quilt before turning it 180° to finish the rest of the vertical anchor lines. See red lines 1–11.

Rotate the quilt 90° to stitch all the horizontal anchor lines between the borders and blocks in the same manner. See blue lines 12–24. You should now have a grid stitched on your quilt that's approximately 6″ apart, plus the extra borders.

Quilting a random crosshatch grid is faster and easier to quilt than a regular, symmetrical grid because you don't have to be exact with your line spacing. Divide and conquer the task by quilting a long line across the quilt wherever there is a seam. This will get most of the quilting out of the way without too much planning or thinking; then you can decide how many more lines you'd like to quilt, and how dense you'd like the quilting to be.

If there are areas of the quilt that do not have any seams to follow (such as borders or large expanses of negative space), you can extend the seamline of the pieced block all the way to the edges. If the pieced blocks are smaller in size, you'll quilt more anchor lines. If the blocks are larger, you can quilt fewer anchor lines.

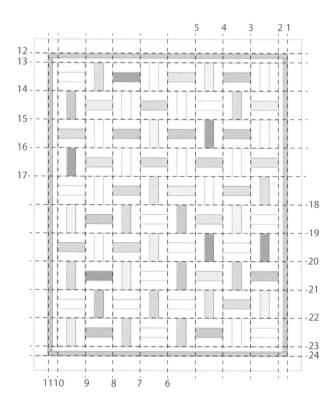

2. Subdivide and quilt another pass of lines to make the grid smaller.

Since the units in this quilt are 2″ finished within each block, the next pass across the quilt could be 2″ intervals in both directions. You can either eyeball the spaces in between each block where there's no seam to follow; or place a piece of painters' tape that's long enough to extend from block seam to block seam. I usually use one piece of tape over and over until it loses its stickiness.

3. Continue quilting straight lines at irregular intervals to complete the design.

This is the fun part, where you get to decide how many lines you'd like to quilt. There's no hard and fast rule since it's a matter of personal preference. I usually quilt another pass in both directions, making the quilted area smaller each time, but random and uneven. Continue to follow the same quilting method; start on the right side of the quilt and work towards the center; rotate the quilt 180°

and continue quilting from the center to the right again, quilting each line from top to bottom across the quilt.

Use a variety of techniques to quilt the lines at random intervals; eyeball the distance between the lines; use the edge of your foot as a guide for spacing; move the needle position to change the distance between your needle and the edge of your foot, or mark some of the lines with painters' tape or a creasing tool.

For best results, quilt one complete pass across the quilt vertically, and then one complete pass horizontally to keep the quilting density relatively even. This also allows you flexibility on when to stop. If you quilt a lot of dense lines in the beginning, you may tire out and not want to continue with the same density across the whole quilt. Dividing and conquering the area one quilting pass at a time also keeps you from getting bored with quilting the same thing over and over. It's a win–win!

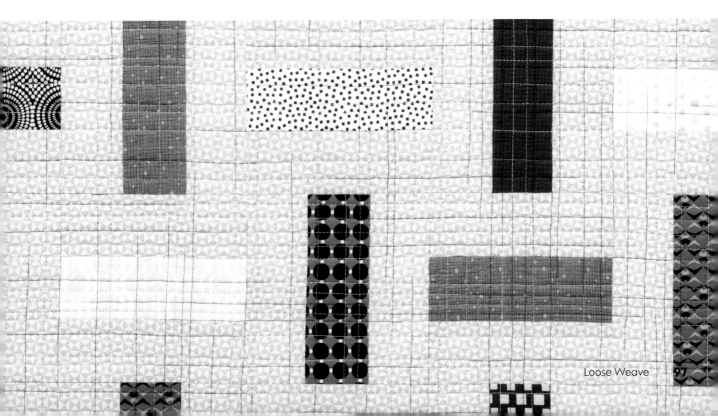

Loose Weave

Free-Motion Quilting Plan: Circuit Board

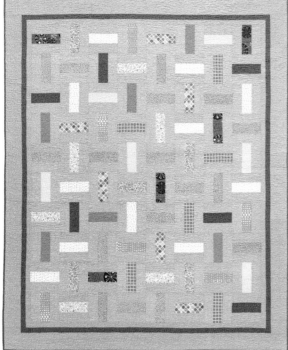

The highly geometric blue, teal, and green prints of this colorway pair nicely with the allover modern vibe of this quilting plan. You can play that up with harsher angles, or add a more breezy, coastal vibe with softer, rounder lines.

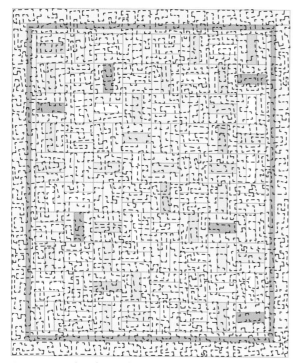

Circuit Board quilting plan.

Because this design is quilted edge to edge, you can start and end each line of quilting randomly in the batting. An allover meander is perfect for hiding inconsistencies in your piecing, especially if the block seams don't line up perfectly.

The Circuits motif takes a little more thinking to not cross over your lines, but even if you do, that's still okay. When it comes to free-motion quilting, there are never any design mistakes, just bonus variations!

1. Start the meandering motif in the upper right-hand corner of the quilt.

Treat the border area just as you would a block section; put the quilt under the machine and begin stitching along the top edge in the batting. Quilt the motif above and to the right of the first block in the corner. Meander your way around the area, covering the border area as well as the first block.

It doesn't matter which direction you stitch first, as long as you fill in the entire area with the quilting design at roughly the same scale. With an allover design, the divide and conquer process occurs as you quilt each block; there is no anchor quilting.

If you aren't sure where to quilt next, stop with the needle down and look at your quilt. Point to the next section you plan to quilt and slowly and methodically stitch your way around the area. Remember to stop with the needle down, shift your hands, and scrunch and smooth the quilt each time you move to a new area to quilt.

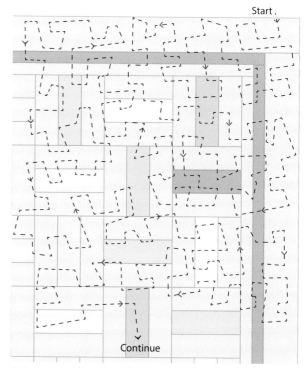

This quilting plan detail is not to scale; yours may vary.

2. Continue quilting block by block, row by row.

Quilt the right-side border and approximately 1–2 rows of blocks. Remember to smoothly stitch in all directions, occasionally quilting a little bit on each adjacent block to blend the quilting. When you complete the quilting on the first vertical row of blocks, you can work your way back up the second vertical row of blocks in the same manner. Or you can cut thread in the batting and start a new row of stitching at the top of the second vertical row of blocks.

TIP Use your hand to hold down the edge of the quilt top as needed.

When quilting near the edges of the borders, be careful that you don't slide the free-motion foot under the fabric. Hold the fabric edges down with one hand to prevent this. You can also decide how dense or loose to quilt and what scale to stitch each motif. A smaller scale is sometimes referred to as "heirloom" machine quilting. I like to stitch about medium size, which I refer to as a "modern" scale.

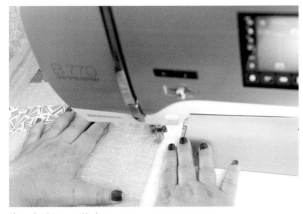

Photo by Susanne Shultis

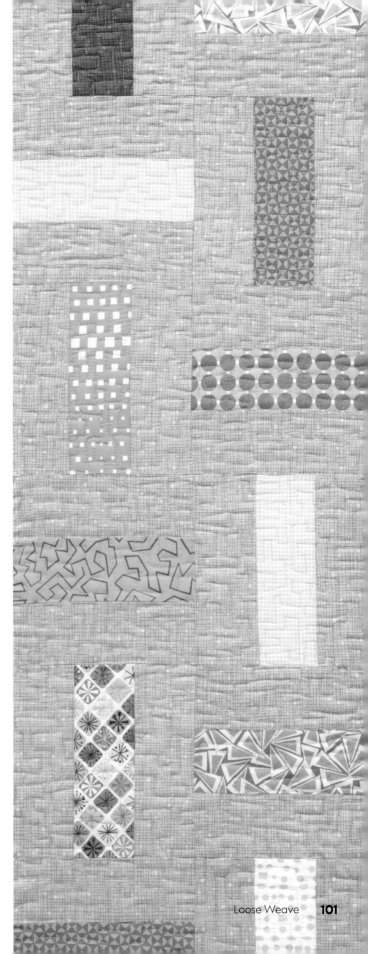

Custom Quilting Plan: Fire & Ice

This custom quilting plan takes advantage of negative space to add dense texture where you'll see it, while minimizing the quilting where you won't. Wavy lines evoke fire on warm hued fabrics, but they could also represent water on cooler colors.

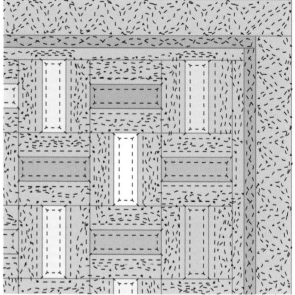

Refer to the quilting plan.

The only stitching in the ditch occurs in the borders and you can decide to quilt those first or last, depending on your comfort level. I prefer to free-motion quilt the inner part of the quilt, with a few pins around the borders for extra stability. After finishing the inner quilt, I quilted the inner borders, and finally the outer borders.

The straight line echo quilting inside of and around each block is done with ruler work, but you can free-motion quilt this free hand for a more whimsical look. By planning how to get in and out of each block area, you'll be able to quilt the entire inside of the quilt (not including borders) continuously. Because you are likely to use more than one bobbin, you'll need to stop and start several times as you quilt your way across the inner quilt. Remember to start and stop in a seam where possible to make this less noticeable.

Detail of fire and ice quilting

1. Free-Motion Quilt Pointy Waves (page 56) and Ruler Lines.

Begin stitching the inner quit in the upper right-hand corner where the inner border and inner background fabric meet. Quilt Wavy Lines (page 38) in any direction as desired until you reach the first rectangle. Then use Ruler Lines to quilt the echoed Jewel Box design (see pages 54–55). If desired, you can quilt another free-motion design in the center of each block, before you make your way back out of the colorful rectangle.

Study the detail photos to see how to make your way around each block. Begin the sequence by stitching wavy lines until you are approximately ¼" away from the corner of a rectangle. Echo quilt straight lines around the outside of the rectangle, backtracking in each of the corners.

Stitch the next set of straight lines in the ditch around the rectangle. Finally, echo ¼" inside of each rectangle, again backtracking as you go to make a continuous line in each corner. Stitch out of any corner to continue with the wavy line design in all directions until you get to the next rectangle.

Repeat the sequence when you get to the next rectangle.

Continue quilting this custom design in a meandering manner; meaning work on one block area at a time methodically until the entire inner quilt is finished.

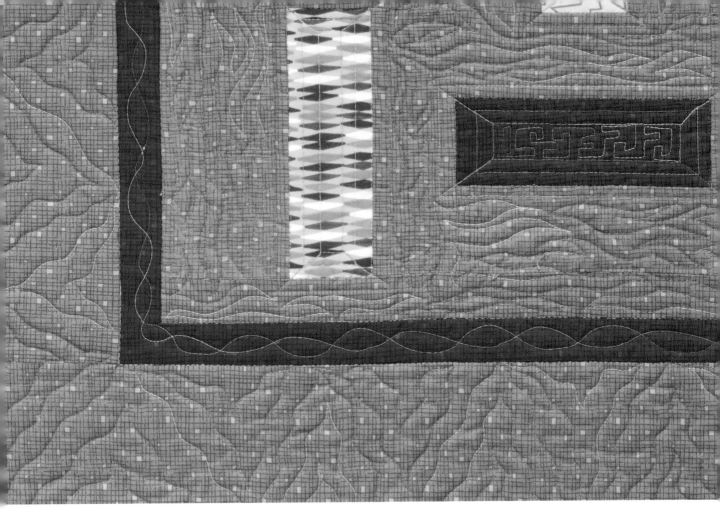

2. Free-motion quilt the Braided Chain design (page 58) in the inner borders.

Begin stitching in one of the seams in the corner of the inner border. For the first pass of the design, quilt a wavy/serpentine line around all 4 borders. When you return to your starting point, cross over each bump that was previously stitched to quilt the second pass of this design. End your stitching at the same starting point, in the seam to hide the stop and start.

3. Quilt Wavy Chevrons (page 57) in the outer borders.

Begin stitching this design off the quilt in the batting, and quilt a diagonal wavy line starting in one of the outer border corners. Quilt an odd number of wavy lines to complete the chevron

motif. Scale this design to roughly fit in between the width of the border fabric. It's okay to stitch near the border edge or slightly off the border edge with each leg of the chevron. The edges will get covered by binding.

Quilt each border strip completely before rotating the quilt and moving on to the next one. Don't try to quilt the same number of chevrons on each side of the border. Instead, begin and end each side of the border with a diagonal line leading into or away from the quilt.

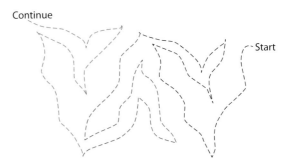

Pinwheel Tessellation

FINISHED BLOCK: 4″× 4″ · FINISHED QUILT: 51″× 62″

A tessellation is a repeating pattern of geometric shapes that tile next to each other, covering a flat area with no gaps or overlapping pieces. Although complex looking, this design is easy to construct as long as you pay careful attention to the color placement. To create the tiling effect for the scrappy-looking version, each rectangle is cut separately so that you can arrange all the units on your design wall before sewing them together. It's a little more tedious to do, but the results of the interesting tessellation are well worth it. Pair up a strip roll and some background fabric and you've got an instant hit!

MATERIALS LIST

Fabric is based on 40″ of usable width.

One precut strip = 2½″ × 40″.

Note: Each precut strip is enough fabric for 2 blocks. If you'd like to make a scrappy version, use 80 half-strips that measure 2½″ × 20″ each.

40 precut strips for blocks (or 1 standard size precut strip roll)*

1 yard of fabric for contrasting background

½ yard of fabric for binding (may be the same as background fabric if desired)

3½ yards of fabric for backing

60″ × 70″ piece of batting

Approximately 1200 yards of thread for machine quilting

*For the 2-color version, choose 1½ yards of dark and 1½ yards of light and cut 20 strips of each.

CUTTING

If cutting fabric from yardage, cut 40 strips, 2½″ × 40″.

From each full-length precut strip

- Cut 8 rectangles 2½″ × 4½″ for a total of 320.

From the contrasting background fabric

- Cut 5 strips 2½″ × 40″.

  Subcut 36 rectangles 2½″ × 4½″.

- Cut 2 strips 7″ × 40″.

  Subcut 10 squares 7″ × 7″.

  Subcut each 7″ square on the diagonal twice to yield a total of 40 side triangles.

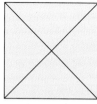

Cut 4 triangles per 7″ square.

From binding fabric

- Cut 6 strips 2″ × 40″ (or wider if desired).

MAKE THE QUILT TOP

Seam allowances are ¼″ and all seams are pressed open.

TIP / **Because the blocks nestle into each other, the rectangle units must be joined separately and sewn row by row, rather than in larger blocks. Take time to plan your layout and take a picture with your camera phone to use as a reference during assembly.**

1. Refer to the quilt top assembly diagram to lay out all the rectangles and setting triangles into a pleasing color arrangement. The layout consists of 8 pinwheel blocks across and 10 blocks down. Background rectangles are placed near the edges of the pinwheel blocks to complete the pattern. The setting triangles are placed around the edges to fill in the gaps.

2. Each tessellated pinwheel consists of 4 rectangles of the same fabric. For best results, arrange your fabrics so that each pinwheel contrasts with the other pinwheels that it touches.

3. Sew 2 rectangles in each diagonal row to create the pieced square units that will tessellate with each block next to it. Take care to ensure each unit is pieced and rotated into proper position.

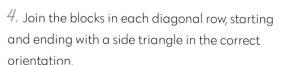

4. Join the blocks in each diagonal row, starting and ending with a side triangle in the correct orientation.

TIP / **Join a side triangle and a block with the tip of the triangle sticking up above the pieced unit as shown. Trim off the triangle tips after each row is sewn.**

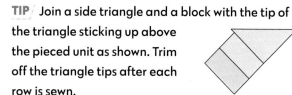

Quilt top assembly

5. Join the rows.

6. Add the top and bottom corner triangles to complete the quilt top.

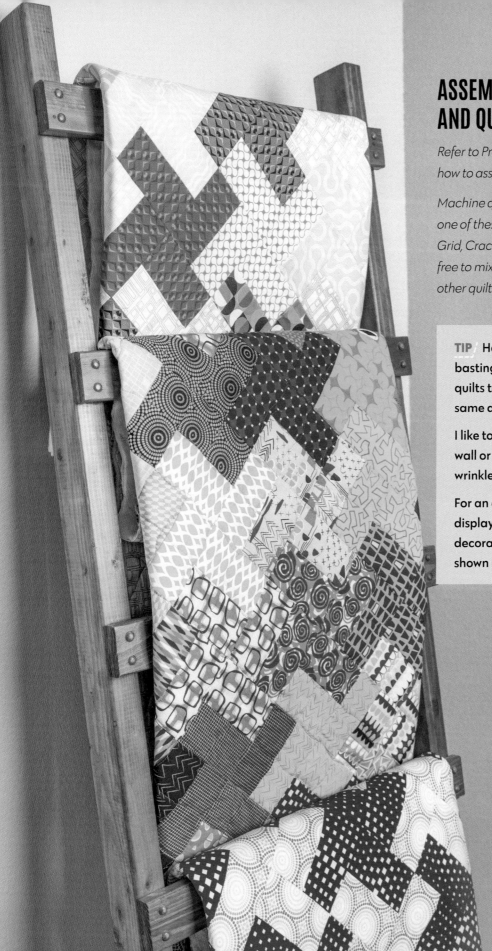

ASSEMBLE THE QUILT LAYERS AND QUILT 3 DIFFERENT WAYS

Refer to Preparing the Quilt (page 22) for how to assemble and baste the quilt layers.

Machine quilt Pinwheel Tessellation using one of these 3 quilting plans: Diagonal Wavy Grid, Crackle Pop!, or Angles & Curves. Feel free to mix and match them on a variety of other quilt patterns, too!

TIP: Have yourself a basting party! (See basting, page 26.) If you have several quilts to make, baste them all on the same day to save yourself some time.

I like to fold my basted quilts over a low wall or railing, so that they don't get wrinkled while I'm waiting to quilt them.

For an added pop of color in your home, display your quilts-in-progress on a decorative quilt ladder, like the one shown here.

Try one of 3 color schemes: light and dark, scrappy, or high contrast.

Walking-Foot Quilting Plan: Diagonal Wavy Grid

Super Scrappy version of Pinwheel Tessellation

This quick and easy quilting plan takes advantage of the fact that most of the quilting will be hidden among the bright and colorful prints. Because the stitching will blend in, "busy" quilts are the perfect canvas for practicing your machine-quilting skills while experimenting with different thread choices.

Diagonal Wavy Grid is quilted much like Random Crosshatch (page 94), but with wavy lines instead of straight lines. The diagonal layout of the quilt lends itself well to diagonal grid quilting. You can decide how closely spaced you want to quilt your grid, and whether you want a more even look or a more random design. I prefer to quilt a looser, less dense design so that you can see the grid.

How Do I Quilt It?

This is a great allover walking-foot plan to quilt when you are short on time because it stitches up super fast and there's absolutely no marking needed! You can quilt the grid in a straight setting, on the diagonal as shown, or at another angle, depending on your pieced design.

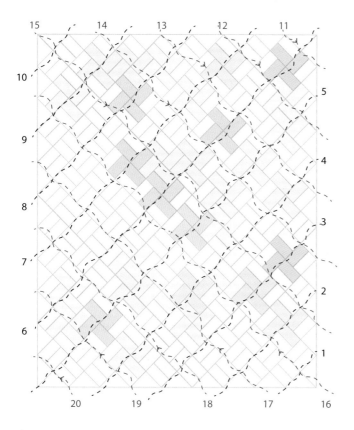

1. Anchor quilt with wavy lines.

Rotate the quilt 45° so that as you quilt, each line will look like it's been quilted diagonally. Stitch wavy lines (page 45) diagonally across all the major seamlines in the quilt to secure it. See the black and red lines in the illustration.

From your perspective, quilt each line from top to bottom (from edge to edge starting and stopping in the batting). Work your way from the right to the middle of the quilt (lines 1–5), cutting the thread at the end of each line of stitching. Rotate the quilt when you've made it about half-way across and continue stitching wavy anchor lines from the middle to the right of the quilt again (lines 6–10). This is the first pass across the quilt in one direction.

Complete the next pass of wavy lines across the quilt in the other direction to complete the grid (lines 11–20). At this point, the lines are roughly 8″ apart.

2. Divide and conquer the quilting!

One pass of lines in both directions is enough to hold your quilt together, but if you prefer denser quilting designs like I do, quilt another pass across the quilt in both directions, subdividing the space in half, so that the grid is approximately 4″ wide (red lines).

As you stitch, roughly follow the seamlines in the pieced blocks to keep your lines going in a diagonal grid. Don't stress about making each line equally distant from every other line, and don't try to quilt the same number of curves in each stitched line. Let your quilting flow organically.

3. Stitch another pass of wavy lines across the quilt in both directions so that the lines are approximately 2″ apart. Continue quilting more densely as desired.

I prefer a tighter grid so my lines are approximately 1″ apart. Anything closer and the lines would start to blur together and lose the overall crosshatch effect. One of the reasons I designed this quilt with extra seams in the background is so that there would be more seamlines to follow while quilting!

Free-Motion Quilting Plan: Crackle Pop!

Color Contrast version of Pinwheel Tessellation

This quilting plan plays up the patriotic color scheme, while giving visual interest to a 3-color quilt. By quilting a dense edge to edge design, the thread still blends in, even when using high-contrast fabric colors in the same quilt. For added sparkle, use a variegated thread color like I did, that includes all the fabric colors in your quilt!

hang of it. Imagine triangle and trapezoid shapes as you stitch. To break this design down block by block, see the Crackle stitch diagram in the Gallery of Free-Motion Designs (page 59).

The beauty of this motif, just like all the designs in this book, is that your stitches will be unique to you. Think how dense or sparse you'd like to quilt, and how long of a line you can stitch before you feel like you are reaching out of control. Backtrack as needed to quilt the next shape.

I recommend visually dividing up the quilt into eight areas of stitching, focusing on one vertical row at a time, including the borders. I usually sketch my quilting plan on a larger scale so that I can visualize the design I'm stitching, but then I end up quilting it with smaller movements, and denser quilting.

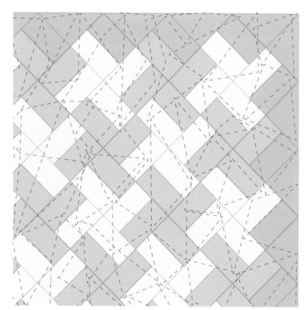

Detail of Crackle Pop! quilting plan

This design is quilted just like the other edge to edge free-motion designs presented in this book. The trick with Crackle though, is to stop often, and figure out where you want to stitch next. It's quilted in short, choppy bursts of lines and it may take a little bit of drawing and quilting practice to get the

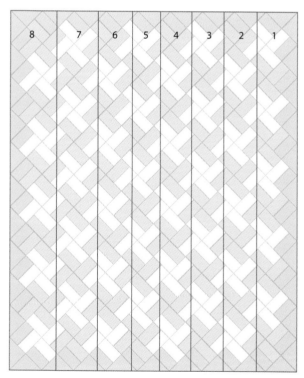

1. Quilt section 1 first.

Begin stitching in the first row of blocks to warm up and then meander your way over to catch the contrasting border as you quilt. Because this design requires a little more thinking, I would quilt smaller sections at a time. You can still blend the design by stitching a little bit into the adjacent blocks. Because of the nested nature of the quilt pattern itself, you end up quilting parts of other blocks as you go.

2. Quilt sections 2–4, then rotate.

You know the drill! Work on one block area at a time, stitching the design from the top of the quilt to the bottom of each row and cutting thread. Remember to stitch in all directions to cover all the areas, and don't forget to smooth out the area just under your hands as you stitch. When you reach the middle of the quilt around row 4, it's time to rotate the quilt 180° so that all the stitched area to your right under the machine, is now off to your left and out of the way.

3. Quilt sections 5–8 to finish.

Continue quilting in a methodical manner, block by block and row by row. As you quilt your way from the center of the quilt to the right edge, you'll have less bulk to deal with, making it easier and easier with each row you stitch.

Custom Quilting Plan: Angles & Curves

Photo by C&T Publishing, Inc.

This custom quilting plan highlights the light/dark contrast in the prints and it's interesting to see how the quilting thread reacts to each. Think of it as a "machine quilting sampler"—a quilt that has lots of room for experimentation and play.

The basic idea is to quilt a different free-motion design in each of the vertical rows. I went a little further and quilted every other row with angular free-motion motifs, while the alternate rows show-case curvy motifs. It's important to try both styles because chances are, you'll gravitate towards one over the other.

Before starting each row of quilting, trace the stitching path you will take to get from block to block without cutting thread. As you try out this quilting plan, feel free to change it up and substitute any of the motifs for any other designs in this book, or even some of your go-to favorites. Due to the busy nature of this quilt, you can't go wrong by adding tons of texture any way you like!

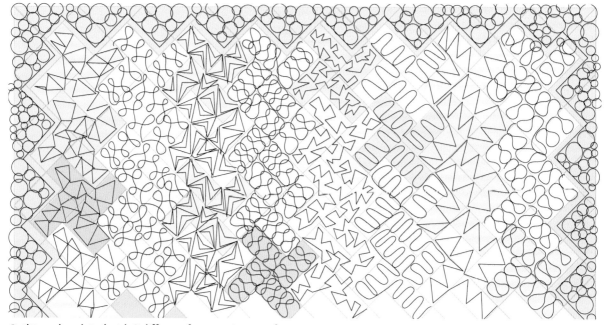

Quilting plan detail with 9 different free-motion motifs

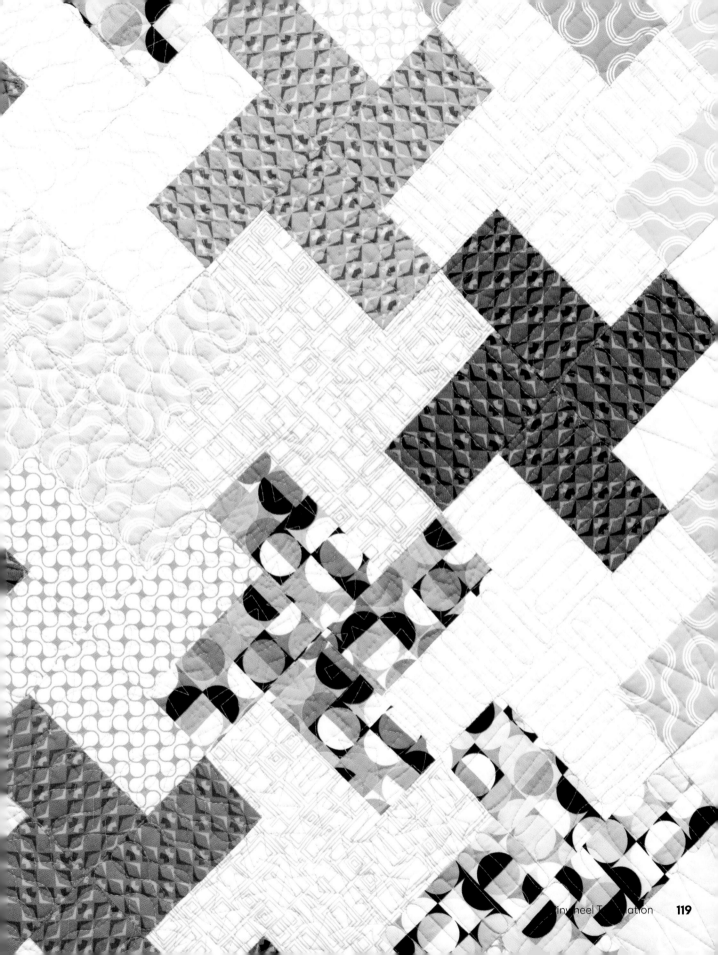

WALKING-FOOT QUILTING

1. Anchor quilt by stitching in the ditch between the rows.

Due to the design of this quilt, I would only stitch around the outline of each of the rows, rather than every seam in the block. This will require more turning of the quilt, but it will help hold the quilt together while you jazz it up with fun free-motion motifs in the blocks.

Follow the SITD (stitch in the ditch) quilting plan to quilt lines all the way around both sides of column 1. Continue quilting each outline to the left of columns 2, 3, and 4. This requires starting and stopping in each column, but once you get into a rhythm, it goes quickly.

Pay attention to the stair step pattern of each outline so you don't stitch too far.

Rotate the quilt to SITD lines between columns 5–8 in the same way. Only rotate the quilt as much as you need to follow the outline.

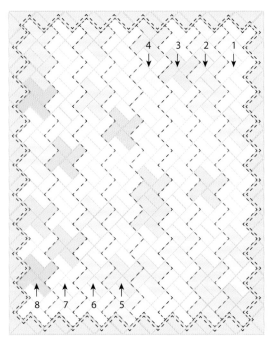

Stitch in the ditch quilting plan

TIP/ If you are comfortable free-motion quilting straight lines with a steady hand, you can choose to stitch the ditches using free-motion techniques instead. In this way, you can quilt the right side of the vertical row from top to bottom but on the alternate rows, you can quilt backwards, back up the other side from bottom to top. If you are really adventurous, you *can* try quilting in reverse with your walking foot to accomplish the same thing, but it's very difficult to keep the lines straight.

2. Echo quilt around the inner quilt.

I call the area of pieced quilt blocks excluding borders the "inner quilt." Finish the walking-foot quilting by echo quilting around the entire inner quilt, approximately ¼″ to ½″ away from the outer block seams. Use the width of your presser foot as a guide for spacing so you don't have to mark any lines.

Depending on the width of your foot, you may need to stitch about 3–5 stitches beyond the corner ditch as you pivot the quilt each time. Start and end the entire echo quilting in the same spot in a seam and rotate the quilt as you quilt around each side of the quilt.

FREE-MOTION QUILTING

1. Draw out your free-motion quilting plan to determine the best stitching path.

You can enlarge and photocopy the full layout of the quilt pattern (page 108) and practice drawing your chosen motifs in each section so that you will know how to make your way in and around each block.

2. Free-motion quilt each row with a different design.

Starting on the right side of the quilt at the top, begin the first free-motion design (see detailed photos below and on page 122).

Quilt an unbroken line of stitching in each block, crossing over each block in the seam where it touches the next block.

3. Free-motion quilt the background area to finish. I quilted pebbles and pebble variations (page 60) because they are very dense. This helps hide the border seams, and dense quilting masks my imperfections!

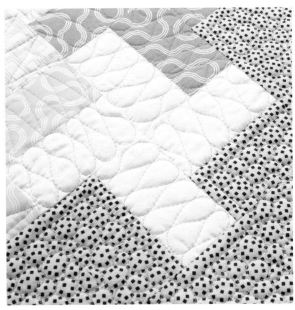

Ribbon Candy quilting (page 61)

Zigzag quilting (page 62)

Photos by C&T Publishing, Inc.

Switchbacks quilting (page 62)

Jagged Stipple quilting (page 51) with Pebbles in the background

Crazy 8's quilting (page 61)

Chevrons quilting (page 57)

Lazy 8's quilting (page 61)

Photos by C&T Publishing, Inc.

Crackle quilting (page 59) with Pebbles in the background

Pebble quilting (page 60)

Binding Your Quilt

When it comes to choosing binding colors, consider whether you want to match the binding to the border or to the background fabric to create a seamless look. Or you may prefer a contrasting fabric that will serve as a frame around the quilt. You can even add a touch of whimsy to your quilt by using up leftover fabrics to piece a scrappy binding.

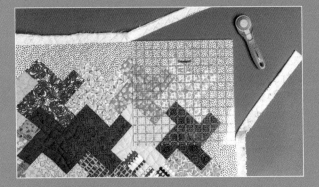

There are two ways to attach the binding, by hand with hidden stitches, or by machine with decorative stitches that become part of the design of the quilt. There's no right or wrong answer—it's all a matter of personal preference.

No matter which method you choose, trim off the excess fabric and batting so that the edges of the quilt are straight and flush. I prefer to use a large square ruler to trim the corners of the quilt, and long straight rulers to trim the edges.

Use your preferred method to make the binding and attach it to the quilt. I always make a standard double fold, hidden seam binding. If you will be finishing by hand, attach the binding to the front of the quilt and if you will be finishing by machine, attach it to the back of the quilt.

FINISH BY HAND

Binding by hand gives the cleanest look and most professional finish. Although it takes longer to accomplish, there's nothing like curling up on the sofa on a cozy evening and stitching away the cares of the day! After sewing the binding to the *front* of the quilt, fold it over to the back side to finish.

For a successful finish, you'll need a sturdy hand sewing needle and thread. Choose a needle that glides through the fabric easily and feels comfortable to grip. I use the same thread that I piece and quilt with and take tiny stitches to secure my seams. You can also double up your thread if needed for extra strength and durability.

1. Thread your needle and trim the thread so it is about 18″ long. Tie a knot on the thread end that you just cut.

2. Tuck the knot underneath the binding, then grab a bite of the backing of the quilt and then a bite of the binding to complete each stitch. For a hidden finish, insert the needle right along the fold of the binding each time. Use a thimble to help push the needle through the quilt if needed.

3. Stitch until the entire binding is secured and stitch past a few stitches from where you began. Tie another knot and pop it through the quilt so it's hidden in the batting.

FINISH BY MACHINE

Attach the binding to the quilt on the *back* of the quilt and fold over the binding to the front and secure it with machine stitches that become part of the design of the quilt.

Option 1: Straight Stitching

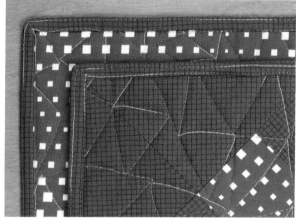

Photo by C&T Publishing, Inc.

Starting anywhere on the right side of the quilt, pull up the bobbin thread to the quilt top. Set your needle position so that you will be stitching just to the right of the folded edge, onto the binding fabric. Hold the top and bobbin threads in place and stitch about 6–8 teeny tiny stitches to secure. Set your stitch length back to normal and stitch next to the folded edge all the way around the perimeter of the quilt. When you get to the corners, stop with the needle in the down position and rotate the quilt to continue stitching. When you get back to the starting point, stitch on top of your previous line of stitches for about 6–8 teeny tiny stitches. Clip thread tails for a smooth finish.

If desired, stitch another straight line of quilting all the way around the perimeter, approximately ³⁄₁₆″ to ¼″ away from the first line of stitching, almost right next to the right edge of the quilt.

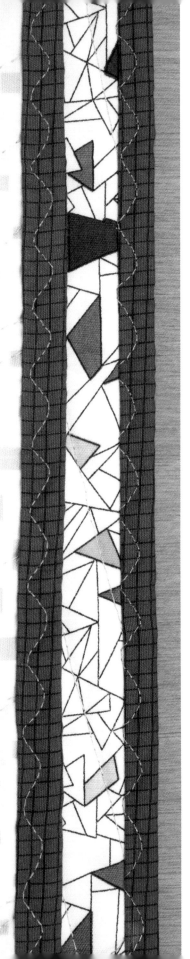

Option 2: Decorative Stitching

Begin stitching anywhere along the edge of your quilt with a decorative stitch (see Quilting Decorative Stitches, page 39). Try to stay within the ¼″ width of the binding fabric as you stitch. Alternatively, you can stitch right next to the ditch or on top of the ditch for a different look. When you get to the corners, stitch slowly so that the decorative stitch can complete its pattern as you rotate and stitch around the corners.

Be sure that the decorative stitching catches the corners on the front and back of the quilt to secure the folds. When you get back to the starting point, stitch on top of your previous line of stitching to secure and clip your thread tails.

Visit my YouTube channel for a video demonstration of my favorite binding methods and my website for step-by-step photo tutorials. (see About the Author, page 127).

Congratulations! You just learned how to finish your own quilts. I hope you enjoy these techniques for many quilts to come!

Appendix

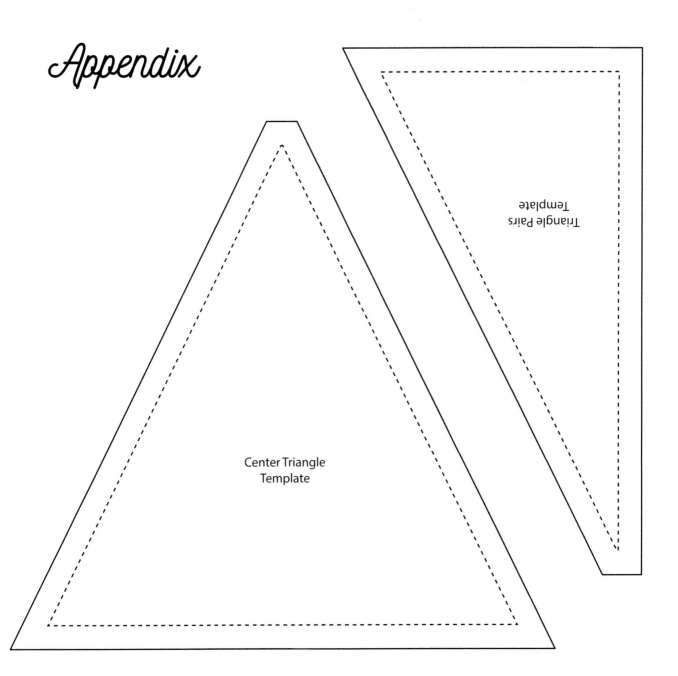

Center Triangle
Template

Triangle Pairs
Template

About the Author

Christa Watson is an award-winning quilter, enthusiastic industry ambassador, modern fabric designer, and author of numerous books, articles, and patterns on piecing and machine quilting. She loves traveling worldwide, teaching others to find joy in making "perfectly imperfect" quilts on a home sewing machine. She lives in fabulous Las Vegas, where she's a busy wife and mom, with three kids who all think it's normal to have a house full of fabric.

VISIT CHRISTA ONLINE AND FOLLOW ON SOCIAL MEDIA!

Website: christaquilts.com

Facebook: /groups/christaquilts

Instagram: @christaquilts

YouTube: ChristaQuilts.TV

Note All the fabrics used to make the 9 quilt projects are from my bold, colorful collections with Benartex. They were machine quilted on my BERNINA 770QE with 50-weight 100% cotton thread from my designer collections with Aurifil. I used Hobbs 80/20 cotton/wool batting in all the quilts.